KILLER WOMEN

NIGEL CAWTHORNE

Quercus

First published in Great Britain in 2018 by Quercus Editions Ltd
This paperback edition published in 2018 by

Quercus Editions Ltd
Carmelite House
50 Victoria Embankment
London EC4Y 0DZ

An Hachette UK company

A CIP catalogue record for this book is available
from the British Library

ISBN 978 1 78648 914 2

10 9 8 7 6 5 4 3 2

Typeset CC Book Production

Printed and bound in Great Britain by Clays Ltd, Elcograf S.p.A.

Nigel Cawthorne is the London-based author of over 200 books, including a number of successful true crime and popular history books. His writing has appeared in over 150 publications.

To my girlfriend, Crystal Nusum.
She has promised not to try it at home.

CONTENTS

The dates cited below refer to the period from the first known murder to conviction and imprisonment – or year of execution.

Belle Gunness Hell's Belle *USA, 1900–08*

Jeanne Weber The Ogress *France, 1905–08*

Martha Rendell Child Poisoner *Australia, 1907–08*

Enriqueta Martí The Vampire of Barcelona *Spain, 1895–1912*

Amy Archer-Gilligan Arsenic and Old Lace *USA, 1907–17*

Tillie Klimek Mrs Bluebeard *USA, 1912–22*

Susan Newell Last Woman to Be Hanged in Scotland *Scotland, 1923*

Vera Renczi Man Slaughterer *Romania, 1920–25*

Bonnie Parker Bonnie & Clyde *USA, 1933–34*

Marie Alexandrine Becker Killer Cougar *Belgium, 1932–36*

Anna Marie Hahn The Blonde Borgia *USA, 1933–37*

Leonarda Cianciulli The Soap-Maker of Correggio *Italy, 1939–40*

Florence Ransom Glamorous Shotgun Assassin *England, 1940*

Margaret 'Bill' Allen Transgender Hammer Murderer *England, 1948*

Rhonda Belle Martin Little Mrs Arsenic *USA, 1937–51*

Caroline Grills Aunt Thally *Australia, 1947–53*

Nannie Doss The Giggling Grandma *USA, 1924–54*

Ruth Ellis Last Woman to Be Hanged in the UK *England, 1955*

Delfina and María de Jesús González The Madams from Hell *Mexico, 1950s–63*

Myra Hindley Moors Murderer *England, 1963–65*

Mary Bell The Tyneside Strangler *England, 1968*

Phoolan Devi The Bandit Queen *India, 1981–83*

Dorothea Puente The Death House Landlady *America, 1982–88*

Maria Gruber, Irene Leidolf, Stephanija Mayer & Waltraud Wagner Lainz Angels of Death *Austria, 1983–89*

Aileen Wuornos The Florida Highway Killer *America, 1989–90*

Beverley Allitt England's Angel of Death *England, 1991*

Kristen Gilbert America's Angel of Death *USA, 1990–96*

Katherine Knight Cannibal Casserole-Maker *Australia, 2000*

KILLER WOMEN

INTRODUCTION

It was Rudyard Kipling who said 'the female of the species is more deadly than the male'. But the statistics do not bear him out. A survey conducted by the United Nations Office on Drugs and Crime in 2013 showed that 96 per cent of perpetrators of homicide worldwide were male. However, there is something uniquely shocking about women who kill, from Myra Hindley to Aileen Wuornos. These women's names have been inscribed on the public imagination. They are the stuff of legend and have inspired books and movies. Female fighters such as Joan of Arc, Boudicca and the Amazons of ancient times have been celebrated. More recently, women in Western and some non-Western societies have taken on leading roles in the military. But that is not what we are dealing with here. The killer women in this book are criminals. Their motives are greed, revenge, sadism, malevolence, sex and sometimes even a perverted form of fun.

Typically, women commit violence against people they know, often husbands, lovers and even their own children. Others turn on the vulnerable or those dependent on their care – relatives, infants, servants and the elderly. Their crimes happen more in private and intimate 'caring' settings than in public. They are dubbed 'hearthside murderers' and, as they appear to be caring for those they kill, they are often given the benefit of the doubt and are allowed to go on and kill again and again.

Analysing the case of Mary Ann Cotton, who may have killed as many as twenty-one, criminologist Dr Elizabeth Yardley said: 'She was constantly creating manifestations of the family that she would then wipe out. This feeds into our expectations of women, that they are carers and nurturers and to a large extent this hasn't changed. It is only recently that we have acknowledged that female serial killers, for example, exist. The FBI still thinks of women who kill as reluctant sidekicks.'

Helena Kennedy QC, who acted for Myra Hindley when she was charged with conspiring to escape from prison in 1974, said: 'We expect women to be better than men – there is that unspoken thing – that we are more shocked when women do terrible things. I feel it myself.'

In her book *Eve Was Framed*, Kennedy explained: 'We feel differently about a woman doing something consciously cruel because of our expectations of the "gentle", nurturing sex. It defies explanation that someone like Myra Hindley, a woman, can stand by and allow torture to take place. Similarly, Mary Bell, the ten-year-old girl who strangled two small children "for fun", perplexed and terrified the British public because her behaviour contradicted the sugar and spice make-up that little girls are supposed to have.'

Women who kill horrify the public and press. Their trials often draw jeering mobs and fill the pages of both tabloids and broadsheets. Everything about them is intensely scrutinized – from their dress-sense to their demeanour. Some protest their innocence to the end. Others are simply cold-blooded criminals who show no remorse. And in some cases, perhaps, the female of the species is more deadly than the male.

ELIZABETH BÁTHORY

The Bloody Countess *Hungary, 1575–1611*

Transylvania is, of course, the home of Dracula – and his supposed model Vlad III Dracula, also known as Vlad the Impaler, who lived there in the fifteenth century. In the sixteenth century, this land of mountains and forests was also home to the legendary beauty Countess Elizabeth Báthory, who lived at Csejthe Castle, a mountain-top fortress overlooking the village of Csejthe below. Hearing rumours of terrible goings-on there, the King of Hungary sent Count George Thurzo, who ruled the province on behalf of the Habsburg Empire, to investigate. When his men arrived at Csejthe Castle, home of Elizabeth Báthory, they 'found one dead girl and another dying of her wounds', according to Thurzo's account in a letter to his wife on 30 December 1610. 'We discovered one, very ill, and covered with wounds, and several others being kept in reserve for the next sacrifice.' After taking depositions from people living in the area, he discovered that the countess had tortured and killed some 650 girls with the assistance of her servants.

E lizabeth Báthory was born in 1560 into one of the oldest and wealthiest families in Transylvania, then part of Hungary. She had many powerful relatives, including a cardinal and several princes; her cousin was prime minister of Hungary and her uncle became King Steven of Poland (1575–86). While she had a strict upbringing on one of her family's many estates, other relatives were rumoured to be insane and sexually perverted, including an uncle said to be an infamous devil-worshipper.

At fifteen, Elizabeth married twenty-six-year-old Count Ferencz

Nádasdy, but kept her surname as it was older and more distinguished than his. They moved to Csejthe Castle. But the count spent much time away from home fighting the Ottomans, earning himself the nom de guerre 'The Black Knight of Hungary'. He was renowned for his imaginative cruelty, playing football with the severed heads of Turkish captives and dancing with their corpses.

During her husband's absence, Elizabeth grew bored. She took a series of young lovers and ran away with one of their servants, a man of reputedly exceptional sexual prowess, but returned and was forgiven by her husband. To keep an eye on Elizabeth, her domineering mother-in-law moved in to the castle. But under the guidance of an old maid named Dorothea Szentes, who claimed to be a witch, Elizabeth Báthory developed an interest in the occult – and soon in far more disturbing activities.

TORTURE AND MURDER

With the aid of her old maid Dorothea Szentes, who was known as Dorka, servant Helena Joo, major-domo Johannes Ujvary and Anna Darvula, another witch who was allegedly Elizabeth's lover, Elizabeth Báthory began to fulfil her sadistic inclinations by disciplining the female servants in an underground torture chamber. Her favourite punishments included leaving them outside naked in the snow, dousing them in cold water until they froze to death, or smearing their nude bodies with honey and leaving them where they would attract bees and insects – a torture it is thought her husband taught her. She would also strip her victims naked, then whip them, or stick pins in the most sensitive places on the victim's body, such as under fingernails.

There was worse. A court chamberlain said he saw the countess cut flesh from one girl and force another to eat it raw. Another was burnt with candles until she died. He also said that he saw her heat up an iron and force it into girls' vaginas.

Then, in 1604, Elizabeth's husband died. The first thing she did was banish her hated mother-in-law. Now there was no one to restrain her. Elizabeth was then forty, vain and eager for fresh young lovers – and soon for young blood.

The tale is told that one day a servant girl accidentally pulled Elizabeth Báthory's hair while combing it. Elizabeth slapped the girl so hard she drew blood and when the blood fell on her own hand, she believed that her skin took on the freshness of that of her young maid. Elizabeth Báthory was convinced that she had found the secret of eternal youth.

She had Johannes Ujvary and Dorka strip the maid, cut her arteries and drain her blood into a vat. Then Elizabeth bathed in it, convinced that it would beautify her entire body.

From then on she regularly bathed in the blood of girls hired as servants from Csejthe and the surrounding villages and she also drank their blood to give her inner beauty. However, as time went on, she began to fear that the treatment might not be as effective as she had hoped. She concluded that the blood of peasant girls was of inferior quality, so she sent out her henchmen to kidnap aristocratic girls.

Although girls hired as servants from the village had been going missing for years, it was only when the daughters of nobility began to disappear that the authorities became concerned. In 1610, villagers saw the dead bodies of four girls being dumped over the ramparts. Then, a girl escaped from the castle and told the authorities about the evil at Castle Csejthe.

King Mathias II of Hungary ordered Elizabeth's cousin, Count Thurzo, to investigate. On the night of 29 December 1610, he raided Castle Csejthe with a band of soldiers. They were horrified by what they found in the castle. One girl lay in the entrance, her body drained of blood. Another, whose body had been pierced with holes, was still alive and they found several girls still alive in the dungeons, some of whom had been tortured. Digging below the castle, the soldiers exhumed the bodies of some fifty girls. And a register of the names of 650 victims was found in Elizabeth Báthory's bedroom.

But as the countess was of noble birth, she was not taken before a court and tried. She refused to plead and was kept under house arrest. However, her accomplices were tried in 1611 at Bitcse. A complete transcript of the trial was made at the time and survives in Hungary to this day.

Johannes Ujvary confessed to being complicit in the murder of thirty-seven girls, six of whom he had personally recruited to work at the castle; Helena Joo confessed to the murder of some fifty-one girls. Victims included her very own sister. Dorka's count was thirty-six. On 7 January 1611, Dorothea Szentes and Helena Joo were sentenced to have their fingers torn off with red-hot pinchers, before being burned alive. Johannes Ujvary was beheaded and his body drained of blood. Anna Darvula, it seems, was already dead.

Although no court ever convicted Countess Elizabeth Báthory of any crime, she did not escape punishment. King Mathias wanted Elizabeth to face the death penalty for her crime, but out of respect for the prime minister, who was her cousin, he agreed to an indefinitely delayed sentence, condemning her to solitary confinement for life. Stonemasons were brought to Castle Csejthe to brick up the windows and doors of the bedchamber with the countess inside, with a small slit left through which food could be passed.

In 1614, four years after she had been walled in, one of the guards wanted a look at this famous beauty. When her food was left untouched, he peeped in. He saw her lying face down on the floor. Elizabeth Báthory, the 'Bloody Countess', was dead at the age of fifty-four.

No doubt the story of Countess Báthory helped fuel the legend of Dracula. Indeed, there were connections between the Báthorys and the Draculas: Prince Steven Báthory had been the commander of the expedition that helped Vlad the Impaler regain his throne in 1476. A Dracula fiefdom, Castle Fagaras, fell into the hands of the Báthorys during Elizabeth's lifetime and both families had a dragon on their family crest.

CANNIBALISM

There is also evidence that cannibalism took place at Castle Csejthe. The local pastor Janos Ponifenus wrote: 'It appears that the flesh of the poor girls was cut up into small pieces, like mushrooms, and served as food to boys. And sometimes, the girls themselves were forced to swallow a grilled hunk of their own flesh. That of some other was cured to serve as food for those who were left. That went on for a long time: sometimes, at night, the bodies of unknown girls were buried in the cemetery; other priests spoke of this among themselves . . .'

MADAME DE BRINVILLIERS

Aristocratic French Poisoner *France, 1666–76*

At seven o'clock on the evening of 17 July 1676, the Marquise de Brinvilliers, barefoot and dressed in the coarse linen shift of the condemned, was led from the Conciergerie Prison in Paris to outside Notre Dame Cathedral. A noose hung around her neck, indicating she was to be executed. She knelt and prayed for forgiveness for the murder of her father and two brothers before being taken to the Place de Grève, where she was beheaded in front of a crowd of some 100,000, including fifty aristocrats – some of whom would later be accused of poisoning too. For now, though, it was only Madame de Brinvilliers who was reviled by her confessor as the 'enemy of the human race'.

Born Marie-Madeleine-Marguérite d'Aubray in 1630, Madame de Brinvilliers was the eldest of five children of Antoine Dreux d'Aubray, who became civil lieutenant of Paris in 1643. In 1665, she married army officer Antoine Gobelin de Brinvilliers, heir to a dye-manufacturing fortune who was later made a marquis. M. de Brinvilliers became friends with roguish cavalry officer Godin de Sainte-Croix. He soon became Mme de Brinvilliers' lover. Her husband did not object as he, too, had a lover. However, her family did.

Mme de Brinvilliers' two brothers made their disapproval plain and her father had her lover Sainte-Croix arrested in March 1663. While imprisoned in the Bastille, he met the famous Italian poisoner Egidio Exili. Released after just six weeks, Sainte-Croix resumed his affair with Mme de Brinvilliers. Incensed by her father, she decided to take her revenge. Sainte-Croix began experimenting with poisons while Mme de Brinvilliers was said to have tested out his concoctions by distributing food laced with them in hospitals, under the guise of an act of charity. However, she later claimed that she obtained the lethal mixture – which she said contained refined arsenic and essence of toads – from King Louis XIV's apothecary-in-ordinary, Christophe Glaser.

Sainte-Croix extorted a high price for the poisons he manufactured – the toxic leaves being imported from Italy – and the de Brinvilliers soon found themselves short of money. Mme de Brinvilliers blamed her husband's extravagance, incompetence with money and gambling. Expecting to inherit under her father's will, she set about slowly poisoning him. For months, he was 'tormented by extraordinary fits of vomiting, inconceivable stomach pain and strange burnings in the entrails'. When he died on 10 September 1666, at the age of sixty-three, his demise was attributed to gout.

Mme de Brinvilliers quickly ran though the money she had inherited, so she resolved to kill her two brothers. The elder had inherited his father's position of civil lieutenant of Paris; the younger was a *conseiller* in *parlement*. Both were wealthy.

Sainte-Croix's valet Jean Hamelin, known as La Chaussée, went to work for her younger brother François who, as luck had it, was unmarried and lived with his elder brother Antoine and his wife. However, Antoine soon spotted that a drink La Chaussée had served him tasted metallic and accused the servant of trying to poison him – La Chaussée declared that the glass must have been used for a purgative and duly removed it.

Then, at Easter in 1670, seven people who had eaten a specially-prepared festive pie fell ill. Antoine was the most severely affected, vomiting frequently and suffering a burning sensation in his stomach. He never recovered and died on 17 June. Again, nothing untoward was suspected.

La Chaussée then started adding poison to François' wine

and food. He suffered the same symptoms as his brother, but also grew impossibly bad tempered, and became incontinent and unbearably smelly. Only his apparently loyal servant La Chaussée would approach him.

Before Antoine had died, he had expressed the suspicion that he was being poisoned. As a result, a post-mortem was carried out. The doctor performing it found signs consistent with poisoning, and yet natural causes could not be ruled out. However, the disease that could cause the symptoms from which both men suffered was so rare, and so unlikely to strike twice, that it became clear it was likely that they had been poisoned.

With her eye on inheriting her brother Antoine's wealth, Mme de Brinvilliers then planned to poison his wife, along with her own sister who made large donations to religious institutions. Her plans were thwarted when Sainte-Croix died. As he was in debt, his property was impounded. Among his things was a casket with a note saying that, in the event of his death, it was to be given to Mme de Brinvilliers. The casket was found to contain a collection of poisons and letters implicating her.

Mme de Brinvilliers fled to England. La Chaussée was tried and found guilty; his punishment was death by torture.

When the French authorities sought to extradite Mme de Brinvilliers, she fled to Holland – France was at war with the Dutch at the time. However, she made the mistake of taking a room in a convent in Liège, an independent city state that had stayed out of the war, though the French had occupied its citadel. Mme de Brinvilliers was arrested and taken to the citadel. In her room, the authorities found a document where she confessed to poisoning her father and brother, along with the five or six attempts on her daughter and husband. In the end, she had thought better of it and nursed them back to health. She also wrote that she had frequently committed incest. Three of her five children were not her husband's, rather Sainte-Croix's or those of an unnamed cousin – she would have had more children had she not used drugs to induce an abortion. She later claimed she had been in the grip of a delirium caused by fever when she wrote this, but it raised the possibilities that she was sexually abused as a child.

While being taken back to France, she tried to commit suicide by swallowing pins and bits of glass, and thrusting a sharpened stick up her vagina. In court, she was confronted with Jean-Bapiste Briancourt, her children's tutor whom she had also taken as a lover. He said that she had told him that she had poisoned her father and brothers, and further intended to kill her sister and sister-in-law. When he demurred, she and Sainte-Croix had planned to kill him too. She rebutted everything Briancourt said and continued to protest her innocence. Nevertheless, on 15 July 1676, the judges found her guilty.

First, she was tortured – stripped naked and tied up, and twenty gallons of water was poured into her mouth through a funnel. As a result, she confessed to everything put to her.

The end was merciful. She was beheaded with a single stroke of a sword. Afterwards, her body was burnt and the ashes thrown to the wind. Before she died, she said: 'Out of so many guilty people must I be the only one to be put to death? ... Half the people in town are involved in this sort of thing, and I could ruin them if I were to talk.'

Eyewitness to the execution

Watching from a window of a house on the Notre Dame Bridge, Marie de Rabutin-Chantal, Marquise de Sévigné said: 'Those who saw the execution say that she has mounted on the scaffold with much courage ... Never has Paris seen such crowds of people. Never has the city been so aroused, so intent on spectacle ...' Mme de Sévigné then noted 'a dull thud, like that of a butcher's cleaver on a block. The executioner had severed her head with one swoop ... "Monsieur," the executioner said, "have I not struck a fine blow? I always commend myself to God upon these occasions and, thus far, he has not failed me."

'She died as she had lived, most resolutely ... A loud murmur went up from the crowd at the final cruelty. But now, at last, it is over and done with. La Brinvilliers has gone up in smoke; her poor little body tossed, after the execution, into a raging fire; and after that her ashes scattered to the wind, so that now we shall be inhaling her ...

'Her confessor called her a saint. The next day, the people went searching through the ashes for La Brinvilliers bones' – presumably seeking them as holy relics.'

CATHERINE MONTVOISIN

La Voisin and the Chambre Ardente *France, 1665–79*

The death of Madame de Brinvilliers was followed by the arrest of a number of alchemists and fortune-tellers also suspected of poisoning. There had been a spate of mysterious deaths among influential members of the nobility and Louis XIV became concerned for the safety of the royal family and members of court, so he reconstituted the *Chambre d'Arsenal*, which had tried cases of heresy in the sixteenth century, as a special tribunal on poisoning and related matters. Meeting in the basement of the Arsenal with the windows draped with black cloth and lit only by flaming torches gave it the unofficial name *Chambre Ardente*, or the Burning Chamber. In the three years of its existence, it issued 319 arrest warrants and sentenced thirty-six people to death. The most famous was Catherine Montvoisin – known as La Voisin – who was burnt at the stake on 22 February 1680.

Overseeing the investigation was Nicolas de La Reynie, the lieutenant general of the Paris Police. During the general crackdown on makeshift laboratories, one name kept coming up. It was La Voisin, who was said to have supplied poisons to ladies who wanted to dispose of their husbands, even administering these 'inheritance potions' herself.

Born Catherine Deshayes in 1640, she was initiated into sorcery at the age of nine, probably by her mother. She married Antoine Montvoisin, whose business as a silk merchant and jeweller led him to bankruptcy. He lapsed into heavy drinking and took his frustrations out on her. To feed her numerous children, she turned to fortune-telling and holding séances dressed in an extravagant red crimson robe, embroidered with 'two hundred and fifty double-headed golden eagles with wings spread'.

Among her clients were people from the highest circles. The Marquis de la Revière noted that La Voisin 'was full of delicious little secrets for the ladies ... which the gentlemen could be grateful for ... La Voisin could make a lady's bosom more bountiful or her mouth more diminutive, and she knew just what to do for a nice girl who had gotten herself into trouble.' At that time, procuring an abortion was a capital offence. And, it was alleged, she provided other services.

La Voisin believed that her occult powers had been given to her by God and argued her case before professors of the Sorbonne. On 12 March 1679, she was arrested leaving an early mass at her parish church, Notre-Dame de Bonne Nouvelle, in the Parisian suburb of Ville-Neuve. Her house, in a secluded section of rue Beauregard, was searched. Locked away in a cabinet was an assortment of powders and philtres, many of which were poisonous. *Grimoires* – black books on Satanism and necromancy – were found, along with robes and other paraphernalia. And in a mysterious oven in a garden pavilion there were fragments of infants' bones. The police also found a long list of her clients.

Other alleged poisoners already in custody were quick to accuse La Voisin. Among them were Marie Bosse who drunkenly boasted that she had become so rich from providing poisons to the rich she was about to retire. La Bosse was sentenced to be burnt alive. Her fourteen-year-old daughter was brought to witness the spectacle in the hope that it would have a salutary effect on her character, while La Bosse's eldest son was hanged for helping his mother prepare the poisons.

Co-conspirator Marie Vigoreux also named Adam du Coeuret, also known as the magician Lesage, a former lover of La Voisin. La Vigoreux died under torture. Lesage had already been sentenced to life in the galleys, but unusually he had been released after a few years. No one knew why. He now told investigator La Reynie of La Voisin's business in abortions and poisons, and said that the small oven in the pavilion was used to burn the bones of infants that were too big to bury in the back garden. He also said that most of La Voisin's clients belonged to the king's entourage. After being interrogated by the *Chambre Ardente*, La Voisin was sentenced to be burnt alive. First she was tortured, but La Reynie complained that the torture had not been applied with the usual rigour and produced no results. Indeed, the night before the execution La Voisin was given a hearty supper, accompanied with a great deal of wine, and began singing bawdy songs. The guards pointed out that, as she was to die the following day, it would be more appropriate if she confined herself to prayer. On 22 February 1680, La Voisin was burnt at the stake.

MADAME DE MONTESPAN

La Voisin's clients included a maid of Françoise-Athénaïs de Montespan, the king's favourite mistress at the time.

When Louis XIV heard of this, he ordered La Reynie to proceed with the interrogation of the witness as quickly as possible, but to record allegations against the Marquise de Montespan on separate folios that were not to be included in the record of the investigation.

Madame de Montespan had been separated from her husband and bore the king eight children whom he legitimized. A patron of Racine and Molière, she was often referred to as 'the king's second wife', or even 'the real queen of France'. In 1671, Louise de La Vallière, the king's official favourite, fell ill. She was thought to have been poisoned. Madame de Montespan was accused, but the matter was hushed up.

Afterwards, La Voisin's daughter Marie revealed that her mother had provided Madame de Montespan with love potions when she feared the king's ardour was waning. La Voisin also held black masses where the naked bodies of Madame de Montespan and other women were used as altars. At one of these ceremonies, Marie claimed, Madame Montespan had said: 'I ask for the friendship of the king . . . that the queen should be sterile and that the king should leave her table and her bed for me; that I should obtain of him all that I ask for myself . . . that the king should leave La Vallière and look at her no more, and that the queen being repudiated, I can marry the king.'

Marie also said that Madame de Montespan and her mother had conspired to kill Louis's new mistress Marie-Angélique de Fontanges, by giving her a pair of poisoned gloves – and the king himself, by presenting him with a petition coated in poison. The Duchess de Fontanges died in 1681, possibly poisoned. Madame de Montespan eventually fell out of favour and withdrew to a convent.

In his confession, Adam Lesage said that child sacrifices had taken place at these black masses. Marie Montvoisin confirmed this with detailed descriptions of the murderous rites. Neither was brought to trial as that would have made their testimony about Madame de Montespan public. Along with other witnesses, they were imprisoned for life on the orders of the king.

DORCAS 'DARKEY' KELLY

Dublin Brothel Keeper *Ireland*, c.*1746–60*

On the wall of Dorcas Kelly's pub in Fishamble Street in Dublin, there is a plaque that reads: 'Previously dubbed the "Maiden Tower" this building was actually an eighteenth-century brothel run by Madam Darkey Kelly, who in 1746 was publicly executed for the alleged murder of her child.' However, recent research has discovered that Dorcas 'Darkey' Kelly was probably Ireland's first serial killer.

Dorcas Kelly was the madam of the Maiden Tower in Copper Alley, off Fishamble Street. She was known as Darkey because the word 'Dorcas' means 'dark' in Irish and because she had long, flowing black hair and coal-black eyes, contrasting with her then-sought-after pale skin.

Taking to prostitution to raise her from the poverty of the time, she was astute enough to use her earnings to purchase the Maiden Tower brothel. It contained a labyrinth of false doors and secret passages that were almost impossible to negotiate unless you were well acquainted with the building. Indeed, some unwanted customers did not escape.

One of Dorcas's clients was the notorious Simon Luttrell, a member of the House of Commons and Sheriff of Dublin. In his younger days, Luttrell was a leading light of Dublin's Hellfire Club, who met in the Eagle Tavern, nearby on Cork Hill.

LUTTRELL, THE DEVIL'S SUCCESSOR

At the Hellfire Club's meetings, a chair was left vacant for the Devil, to whom the first toast of the proceedings was always made. The club also had a huge black cat, said to be the Devil incarnate, which was served first at dinner.

The poem *The Diaboliad*, dedicated to 'the worst man in His Majesty's dominions', was thought to be about Luttrell. In it, the ageing Devil and his cohort leave hell to search Earth for a successor. They gather politicians, courtiers and 'lordlings from the arms of whores' and take them back to hell. There the Devil insists that the next person to occupy his throne must be:

> False to God, who every law defied,
> Thief, traitor, hypocrite and parricide;
> Let him who claims these titles as his own
> Come forward, prove his claim and take the crown.

Luttrell steps forward. All the other notorious libertines of the day were considered and found wanting. Only Luttrell was thought bad enough to take over. Luttrell was also said to have made a pact with the Devil and held black masses where, once, a dwarf was sacrificed. A biography of the Eton-educated Luttrell published in 1769, while he was still alive, stated: 'The name of Luttrell has come to mean in Ireland, traitor, villain, bastard, coward and profligate, and everything that can be conceived as odious and horrible.' He was also known as the 'King of Hell'.

Dorcas Kelly accused Luttrell of fathering her baby to blackmail him into providing financial support. He responded by accusing her of being a witch and of killing the supposed child in a satanic ritual, though no body was found. Dorcas was said to have been executed in 1746. However, researchers have found newspaper reports from the time that say when the Maiden Tower was searched, the bodies of five men were found in a dungeon there.

On 17 March 1760, Dorcas Kelly was tried for the murder of John Dowling, a local shoemaker. Found guilty, she was sentenced to death, but she challenged the sentence on the grounds that she was pregnant. A jury of matrons was then sworn in. They found that she was not with child. Her sentence was carried out on 7 January 1761: first half-hanging her in Baggot Street, at the time known as Gallows Road for its hangings, then burning her while she was still alive.

The custom at the time was to bury the remains in a pit beside the gallows. But after Dorcas 'Darkey' Kelly was executed, the local prostitutes rioted. They seized what was left of her body and broke open her former brothel in Copper Alley to hold a wake. Thirteen of them were arrested and sent to Newgate prison.

SOPHIE CHARLOTTE ELISABETH URSINUS

Aristocratic Arsenic Poisoner *Prussia, 1797–1803*

In early May 1803, Sophie Ursinus, the wealthy widow of a privy counsellor, was playing whist at a party in Berlin when a footman came to tell her that several police officers were waiting in an anteroom and wanted to speak with her. She rose without emotion, put down her cards and apologized to the other players for the interruption. Doubtless there had been a mistake that would soon be cleared up and she would return soon. She did not. To the consternation of her companions, she faced criminal charges and had been taken to prison.

The previous February, her servant Benjamin Klein complained of feeling unwell. His mistress gave him a cup of broth and, a few days later, some currants. These remedies were no help. Indeed, he got worse.

On 28 February, she gave him some rice. When he refused it, she threw it away. This aroused his suspicion. He searched her rooms and found a bottle containing powder labelled arsenic. On 22 March, she offered him some plums which he gave to a maid whose brother was an apprentice in a chemist's shop. When analysed, they were found to contain arsenic. The chemist went to the authorities and Frau Ursinus was arrested. The police then began looking into the suspicious deaths of her husband three years earlier, her aunt, aged spinster Christiane Witte, and a Dutch officer named Rogay, thought at one time to have been her lover.

While admitting that she had tried to poison Klein, Frau Ursinus denied all other charges.

Born Sophie Charlotte Elisabeth Weingarten on 5 May 1760, she was the daughter of Baron von Weingarten, former secretary to the Austrian legation in Prussia, who had defected after important Austrian government papers had been stolen by his mother-in-law, an enthusiastic supporter of Frederick the Great. She lived with her parents until the age of twelve, when she was sent to be educated by her married sister in Spandau. There she underwent a profound change, rejecting the Catholic faith of her parents and becoming a Lutheran. Then, after a love affair that her family thought unsuitable, she returned to her parent's home in Stendal.

At the age of eighteen, she met her future husband, Theodor Ursinus, who was then a counsellor of the Supreme Court. Although she did not exactly love this grave, sickly, elderly man, she admitted a certain affection for him and, after a year, consented to marry him because of his many excellent qualities, his position and his prospects.

After he was promoted privy counsellor, they moved to Berlin where he died on 11 September 1800. The marriage had not been a happy one. The couple were childless and lived more or less separately. It was said that Frau Ursinus was 'inclined to flirtation' and had taken a strong fancy to the Dutchman Rogay. Her aged husband did not disapprove of the attachment, which she maintained was platonic. This was generally believed as it was thought that the phlegmatic Dutchman was incapable of the 'grand passion'.

Rogay left Berlin for a time. When he returned he suddenly died, three years before Frau Ursinus's husband also succumbed. Once it was known that Frau Ursinus had a propensity for arsenic, she was charged with his murder. However, two competent physicians swore that Rogay died of consumption – that is, tuberculosis – and she was acquitted on that charge.

Next the police investigated the death of her husband. According to her statement, she had given a small party on 10 September, her husband's birthday. He had been in fairly good spirits, but had remarked more than once that he feared he was not long for this life. There was nothing wrong with him when he retired for the night. However, in the middle of the night his moans and groans awakened her. There was an emetic by the bedside which, she said, the doctor had prepared for him. Although she wanted him to take it, she gave him an elixir instead. When he felt no better, she tried the emetic, then rang for the servants. None came. She went to look for the porter, but could not find him. So, she remained alone with her ailing husband. In the morning he was very weak and he died that afternoon.

The prosecution alleged that she had made no real effort to summon the servants and the family physician said that he had not prescribed an emetic. Frau Ursinus admitted buying arsenic, saying that she was going to use it to kill rats. There were no rats in the house.

Herr Ursinus's body was exhumed. The two doctors performing the post-mortem could not find positive traces of arsenic, though from the general condition of the body they could not rule it out. However, the three physicians who had attended Herr Ursinus in his last illness insisted that he had died from natural causes.

Next the police investigated the death of Frau Ursinus's maiden aunt who died on 23 January 1801. Frau Ursinus had arrived at her aunt's house in Charlottenburg on the 16th. Fräulein Witte was already ill and the following day she took a turn for the worse. Frau Ursinus called a doctor. Nevertheless, her aunt's condition deteriorated. Another doctor was called on the 23rd. He said that the illness was not concerning, but that night Fräulein Witte died. Frau Ursinus was left a considerable inheritance.

During the trial it came out that, during a previous visit to Charlottenburg, Frau Ursinus had written to a chemist in Berlin, ordering arsenic to kill the rats in her aunt's house. Again, there were no rats and Frau Ursinus was convicted of murder. She was also convicted of the attempted murder of her manservant Benjamin Klein, which she admitted. But no motive was found. It was thought that he was privy to her secrets and was intending to leave her service. Klein recovered and survived another twenty-three years, living comfortably on a pension she was ordered to pay.

Punishment

Frau Ursinus was sentenced to life imprisonment in a fortress in Glatz in the Prussian province of Lower Silesia (now Kłodzko in Poland). However, she was allowed to furnish her own apartments and had a ladies' maid. Dressed in silk and satin, she was allowed to have parties. At one, a guest noticed some grains of sugar in a salad and shied away.

'Don't be afraid,' Frau Ursinus said. 'It's not arsenic.'

She died on 4 April 1836 and was buried in an expensive oak coffin she had bought a year earlier. She was laid out in a white petticoat, a cap trimmed with pale blue ribbon and white gloves. On one finger, she wore a ring that had belonged to her late husband and had his portrait clutched to her breast. She was the first person to be buried in the Protestant cemetery that King Frederick William III had given to the evangelical congregation at Glatz.

The funeral was attended by coaches full of friends and acquaintances, along with a choir. Half her fortune was left to her relatives. The rest was given to the poor and charities. Her jailer was also provided with a legacy and his daughter was given a piano.

ANNA MARIA ZWANZIGER

The German Brinvilliers *Bavaria, 1808–09*

Working as a housekeeper, Anna Zwanziger took a peculiar delight in poisoning her employers and other members of the household. When apprehended carrying arsenic, she could hardly throw herself on the mercy of the courts as her employers had been judges. After confessing her crimes, she was beheaded.

Although she was compared to Madame de Brinvilliers, Anna Zwanziger was no aristocrat. Born in 1760, she was the daughter of an innkeeper in Nuremberg and orphaned at the age of five. She was passed around members of the family until, at the age of ten, she was taken in by a wealthy merchant who gave her a good education. However, at fifteen, her guardian decided to marry her off to a thirty-year-old lawyer. The man was a drunk and she worked as a prostitute to support him and their two children, though she maintained that she was picky about her clients.

'I always had the delicacy to admit none but men of rank and discretion,' she said, 'for from my youth upwards my principle has ever been to stick to those who could advance my fortunes; and thus, I had the good luck to receive a great deal of assistance from many distinguished men.'

These included senior members of the judiciary. A scandalous affair with an aristocratic lieutenant led her to leave her husband. But she returned and the day after they divorced she remarried him.

She was thirty-six when her husband died after a short illness.

There were suspicions that she had poisoned him. In Vienna, she tried to establish herself as a confectioner. When this failed, she became a housekeeper. An affair with a clerk in the Hungarian exchequer resulted in an illegitimate child, which was sent to a foundling hospital, where it died soon after.

After returning to Nuremberg, she became the mistress of a Freiherr von W—, supplementing her income making dolls. After three months she got a better offer from a minister resident in Frankfurt who needed a housekeeper. She soon lost that job due to her dirty habits and poor cooking. There was a succession of other short-lived jobs, before she returned to her lover in Nuremberg. But he was a married man and cooled towards her when she told him she was pregnant. By then he was having an affair with an actress. Zwanziger then had a miscarriage and attempted suicide. She also took her revenge on her errant lover by sending his letters to his wife. A second failed suicide attempt followed and her lover gave her money to leave Nuremberg.

'It is all Freiherr von W—'s fault that my heart is so hard,' she said. 'When I opened my veins and he saw my blood, he only laughed. And when I reproached him with having once before ruined a poor girl who drowned herself and her child by him, he laughed again. My feelings were terrible, and when I afterwards did anything wicked, I said to myself, "No one ever pitied me, and therefore I will show no pity to others."'

After a period of ill-health, she returned to housekeeping, supplementing her wages by stealing. Seeking refuge with her son-in-law in Mainbernheim, she was thrown out when he read in the newspaper that she was wanted for theft. In the town of Neumarkt, she taught sewing to young girls and made the acquaintanceship of an elderly general. When she got over-familiar, he fled to Munich. She followed only to be given some money to go away. Again, she returned to prostitution. The pickings were slim as she was now nearing fifty.

Reverting to her maiden name Schönleben, she got a job as a housekeeper with Justice Wolfgang Glaser, who had separated from his wife. The wife returned, only to die shortly afterwards. Anna Schönleben moved on to become housekeeper to Justice Grohmann, who was thirty-eight and intending to marry the daughter of another judge. He was often bedridden with gout and Zwanziger nursed him. In the spring of 1809, his condition suddenly grew worse and, after eleven days, he died.

Zwanziger next became housekeeper to a magistrate named Gebhard and nursemaid to his wife who was heavily pregnant. On the seventh day after giving birth, Frau Gebhard died in agony, saying: 'Merciful heaven! You have given me poison.'

Three months later guests having dinner with Gebhard fell ill. A messenger given a glass of wine at the house suffered the same symptoms. The messenger's nineteen-year-old porter was also given a glass of brandy. After a sip, he saw a white sediment in it and drank no more. Nevertheless, he was violently sick. So was a maid, whom Zwanziger had fallen out with and made the mistake of accepting a cup of coffee from her.

Gebhard had five friends round to play skittles. They drank some beer from his cellar and all of them fell ill. Zwanziger was dismissed. Before she left, she refilled the salt-box, which was not normally part of her duties. Two maidservants who commented on this were given cups of coffee with some additive Zwanziger poured from a wrap of paper. The child was given a biscuit soaked in milk.

Soon after Zwanziger left, they became ill. Gebhard had the contents of the salt-box and the salt-barrel analysed and found they contained a high proportion of arsenic. He reported this to the authorities. Bodies of other victims were exhumed and traces of arsenic found.

Meanwhile Zwanziger wrote to Gebhard, warning his dead baby would miss her, and to Glaser, offering her services again. When she returned to Nuremberg on 18 October 1809, she was arrested and found to be carrying a packet of arsenic and two packets of the toxic medicine tartar emetic in her pocket. For six months, she denied everything. But when confronted with the evidence against her in court on 16 April 1810, she collapsed and confessed to killing Glaser's wife and poisoning several members of his household and visitors who survived. Grohmann and his guests got similar treatment, though she denied poisoning Grohman deliberately.

'Grohmann may have drunk some poisoned beer,' she said. 'But Grohmann was much too valuable to me that I should injure him purposely; he was everything to me; and what he ate, that I ate too. He was my best friend, and never offended me, so that I had nothing to revenge upon him.'

She also confessed to murdering Madame Gebhard, deciding to do so four days before she had given birth.

'Madame Gebhard was very cross, treated me roughly and scolded me for having, as she said, neglected the housekeeping,' Zwanziger said. 'I resolved to poison her.'

She claimed that this was not to kill her, 'but only to plague her by making her sick, because she had plagued me ... Had I thought that Madame Gebhard died by my fault, I would have laid myself in the grave beside her.'

As for the others: 'I must confess that it was good fun to see people who had teased me made very sick.' And when she left the Gebhard household, 'I mixed the contents of the salt-box which is used in the kitchen with arsenic, in order that after I was gone everybody who stayed in the house might get some of it, and also to get the maid into trouble ... [I] dropped the arsenic into it while I stirred the salt three times, and made some joke about it.'

She said she had not meant to kill Gebhard's child either, just make it cry so that he would call her back. On 7 July 1811, Zwanziger was sentenced to being beheaded by the sword and her body exposed on a wheel, which was remitted. Accepting the sentence, she said it was a good thing for mankind as it would have been impossible for her to stop poisoning. She also thanked the judge for his kindness and asked his permission to appear to him after death to demonstrate the immortality of the soul.

A professional view

Bavarian legal scholar and progenitor of modern criminal psychology Paul Johann Anselm Ritter von Feuerbach included a study of the Zwanziger case in his book *Narratives of Remarkable Criminal Trials*, calling the chapter 'The German Brinvilliers'. In it, he said:

> Her attachment to poison was based upon the proud consciousness of possessing a power which enabled her to break through every restraint, to attain every object, to gratify every inclination, and to determine the very existence of others. Poison was the magic wand with which she ruled those whom she outwardly obeyed, and opened the way to her fondest hopes. Poison enabled her to deal out death, sickness, and torture to all who offended her or stood in her way – it punished every slight – it prevented the return of unwelcome guests – it disturbed those social pleasures which it galled her not to shine – it afforded her amusement by the contortions of the victims, and an opportunity of ingratiating herself by affected sympathy with their sufferings – it was the means of throwing suspicion upon innocent persons, and of getting fellow-servants into trouble. If she flattered herself with the prospect of marrying an already married man, at her will wives descended into the grave, and left their husbands free for her. She grudged the bride her bridegroom, and the wedding-feast was held in vain. In time mixing and giving poison became her constant occupation; she practised it in jest and in

earnest, and at last with real passion for poison itself, without reference to the object for which it was given. She grew to love it from long habit and from gratitude for its faithful services, she looked upon it as her truest friend, and made it her constant companion ...

MARIE LAFARGE

The Triumph of Science *France, 1840*

Charged with poisoning her husband, the case of Marie Lafarge became a *cause célèbre* in France in the 1840s. It seemed certain that she would be acquitted when two doctors found no arsenic in her victim's body. But then a leading forensic toxicologist repeated the tests using a new method of detection developed in England by James Marsh. To the horror of her supporters, Marie Lafarge was convicted.

Marie Lafarge was well connected. Her father, Colonel Capelle, had been a member of Napoleon's Guard and was a close friend of many of the nobles of the First Empire. But both her father and mother died while she was young. Fostered by an aunt, she was sent to the best schools. But when she came of age, her aunt and uncle were eager to marry their ward off.

A proposal came from an iron-master named Charles Lafarge. To Marie, he was of an inferior social class, but he had a château – the thirteen-century former Carthusian monastery of Glandier set in a large estate in the south of France, where he lived with his mother and sister. They had known each other just five days when they married. However, when they reach Glandier in August 1839, Marie found the château was dilapidated and surrounded by the chimneys of rundown ironworks built on the estate.

Locking herself in her room, she wrote a letter to her husband, begging to be released from her vows, saying: 'Charles, – I am about to implore pardon on my knees. I have betrayed you culpably. I love you not, but another ... Get two horses ready. I will ride to Bordeaux and then take a ship to Smyrna. I will leave you all my possessions. May God turn them to your advantage, you deserve it. As for me I will live by my own exertions. Let no one know that I ever existed ...'

She went on to say, crucially: 'If this does not satisfy you, I will take arsenic, I have some ...' And she concluded: 'Spare me, be the guardian angel of a poor orphan girl, or, if you choose, slay me, and say I killed myself. Marie.'

Later she admitted that she did not have a lover and withdrew her plea, writing to her uncle: 'I have accepted my position, although it is difficult. But with a little strength of mind, with patience, and my husband's love, I may grow contented. Charles adores me and I cannot but be touched by the caresses lavished on me.'

To another she wrote that, under a tough exterior, her husband had a noble heart, while his family overwhelmed her with their attentions and she had settled down to her domestic duties. As part of their reconciliation, the couple wrote wills in each other's favour. However, unbeknownst to Marie, Lafarge made a second will, nullifying the first and favouring his mother and sister.

Lafarge had been developing an innovation in iron smelting and sought to use his wife's dowry to exploit it. He headed for Paris to raise more money from her relatives. While they were parted, they sent each other affectionate letters. Marie also had a portrait painted to send to her husband. It was to be accompanied by some small cakes made by his mother, who also wrote a letter at Marie's request, asking him to eat one at a particular hour. Marie would eat one at the same time, it said, securing a mystical bond between them. However, when the package arrived on 18 December, Lafarge opened it to find one large cake instead of several small ones. Nevertheless, at the appointed time, he ate a piece of it and became violently ill. It was noted later that, two days before the package had been sent, Marie had bought arsenic from a local chemist, saying she wanted to kill the rats that were infesting the old house. When she heard that her husband had been taken ill, Marie was convinced that he was going to die and became agitated.

However, Lafarge recovered and returned to Glandier on 5 January 1840. That same day Marie ordered more arsenic from the chemist. Lafarge soon became ill again. The dutiful Marie was constantly by his bedside and sought to take sole charge of his nursing. This caused suspicion in the household. Her mother-in-law's companion Anna Brun said that she saw Marie mixing white powder into her husband's food and medicine, and when she gave him a drink, he cried out: 'What have you given me? It burns like fire.'

Marie dismissed this as inflammation of the stomach because of the wine he continued drinking. His mother also spotted white powder floating on the chicken broth Marie had prepared and showed it to the doctor – he said it was lime falling from the white-washed walls.

A new doctor was summoned. He sent some of the white powder for chemical analysis, but no arsenic was detected. Nevertheless, Lafarge's mother accused Marie of being a murderess as her son was now dying. From then on, Lafarge would not take any food or drink from Marie and could not stand the sight of her. On 14 January, less than ten days since he had returned from Paris, he died.

A post-mortem was ordered and arsenic was found. Marie was arrested and jailed. The newspapers took an intense interest in the case and soon uncovered a story from her past. Some jewels had gone missing when Marie visited an old school friend, the Vicomtesse de Léautaud at the Château de Busagny – and the vicomte now sought to prosecute Marie. The jewels were found in a search of Glandier. Marie admitted to having them, but claimed, at first, that she was honour-bound to remain silent about how she had got them. At the behest of her lawyers, Marie wrote to the Vicomtesse de Léautaud, begging her to tell the truth about the jewels.

MARIE'S LETTER TO VICOMTESSE DE LÉAUTAUD

Marie [de Léautaud], – May God never visit upon you the evil you have done me. Alas, I know you to be really good, but weak. You have told yourself that as I am likely to be convicted of an atrocious crime I may as well take the blame for one which is only infamous. I kept our secret. I left my honour in your hands, and you have not chosen to absolve me.

The time has arrived for doing me justice. Marie, for your conscience's sake, for the sake of your past, save me! . . . Remember the facts; you cannot deny them. From the moment I knew you I was deep in your confidence, and I heard the story of that intrigue, begun at school and continued at Busagny by letters that passed through my hands.

You soon discovered that this handsome Spaniard had neither fortune nor family. You forbade him to love, although you had first sought his love, and then you entered into another love affair with M. de Léautaud . . . The man you flouted cried for vengeance . . . The situation became intolerable, but money alone could end it. I came to Busagny, and it was arranged between us that you should entrust your diamonds to me, so that I might raise money on them, with which you could pay the price he demanded . . .

Remember I have all the proofs in my hands. Your letters to him and his to you, your letters to me . . . Your letter, in which you tell me that he is singing in the chorus at the opera, and is of the stamp of man to extort blackmail . . . There is one thing for you to do now. Acknowledge in writing under your own hand, dated June, that you consigned the diamonds to my care with authority to sell them if I thought it advisable. This will end the affair.

When her friend refused to come to her aid, Marie told the judge that, before the vicomtesse was married, she had an affair with a penniless Spaniard who subsequently blackmailed her. The vicomtesse had given Marie the jewels to sell to get the money to pay him off. Without the vicomtesse's corroboration of this story, Marie was convicted of theft and sentenced to two years.

In the murder trial that followed, the defence realized that the case hinged on the autopsy tests that found arsenic. Samples of the contents of the stomach preserved from the post-mortem were tested again at the behest of the prosecution. This time no arsenic was found. The prosecutor then had Lafarge's body exhumed. Again, no arsenic was found. However, when a sample of eggnog Marie had given Lafarge was also tested, chemists found enough arsenic to poison ten men. To settle the matter, the prosecution called in France's leading toxicologist Mathieu Orfila, an acknowledged expert on the recently introduced Marsh test. He tested a sample from the body and this time arsenic was found.

Although controversy continued, Marie Lafarge was convicted of murder and sentenced to life with hard labour. King Louis-Philippe commuted this to life without hard labour. Writer George Sand rallied to Marie's defence and Orfila's opponent François Vincent Raspail wrote scathing pamphlets demanding her release. But Orfila countered with public lectures on the Marsh test. Meanwhile, Marie wrote her *Mémoires* in prison. She was released by Napoleon III in June 1852, but was already suffering from tuberculosis and died five months later.

DETECTING ARSENIC – THE MARSH TEST

From the late eighteenth century, chemists had been able to detect arsenic – or at least arsenic trioxide, the form favoured by poisoners. However, the early tests were not very accurate and arsenic is surprisingly common. It occurs in the earth and can seep into an unsealed coffin, so its detection using those early methods was not very useful to forensic scientists.

In 1832, James Marsh, a chemist at the Royal Arsenal in Woolwich, was called in by the prosecution in a poisoning case. Using the standard method of detecting arsenic, he passed hydrogen sulphide through the suspect sample. A yellow precipitate showed the presence of arsenic, but this did not keep well and, by the time it was presented in court, there was not enough of it to convince the jury.

Marsh was frustrated by this, particularly as the culprit, though acquitted, later confessed. So he set about developing a more accurate test. In a glass vessel, he would mix the sample with zinc and acid. If arsenic was present, arsine gas would be produced, along with hydrogen. This was burnt, producing a silvery-black mirror of arsenic deposited on the inside of the glass. Comparing this with the film produced by known amounts of arsenic, it was possible to measure the amount of arsenic in the sample. Marsh published his results in 1836.

MARIE MANNING

The Bermondsey Horror *England, 1849*

Recording the hanging of Marie Manning and her husband outside Horsemonger Lane Gaol in London, *The Times* of 14 November 1849 called her: 'Lady Macbeth on the Bermondsey stage . . . Jezebel, the daring foreigner, the profane unbeliever, as Maria Manning now seems to have been; the ready arguer, the greedy aggrandizer, the forger, the intriguer, the resolute, the painted and attired even unto death.'

The police were looking for Irish customs officer and money-lender Patrick O'Connor who had gone missing. On 8 August 1849, he had been for dinner at the home of Mr and Mrs Manning at 3 Miniver Place, Bermondsey, so friends visited the house looking for O'Connor, discovering that the Mannings had disappeared and reported their suspicions to the police.

Two constables were sent to dig up the garden at Miniver Place. They noticed that mortar between the flagstones in the kitchen was still damp. Prizing up the flagstones they found O'Connor's body, naked and bound. His skull was fractured in two places and a bullet protruded under the skin over his right eye. The hunt for the Mannings was on.

The police believed the Mannings were on a ship from London to New York – it was stopped and boarded, only for the police to find another couple with the name among the passengers. A cabman then came forward saying that he had taken Marie Manning to King's Cross Station. There, she had bought a ticket for Edinburgh. In Edinburgh, she had already been arrested for trying to sell some of O'Connor's railway stock, taken from among his possessions. The Edinburgh stockbrokers were suspicious of her foreign accent – Marie was Swiss – and were warned that some railway stock had been stolen in London.

Frederick Manning, a publican and suspected thief, was out trying to sell the couple's furniture when Marie made off. He was arrested the following week in Jersey after being spotted by a man who had known him in London and had read about the 'Bermondsey Horror' in the newspapers. When he was arrested, he told the police that Marie had shot O'Connor.

'I never liked him,' he explained. 'So I battered his head with a ripping chisel' – that is, a crowbar. Both were charged with murder.

At their trial at the Old Bailey on 25 and 26 October 1849, Marie turned on her husband: 'The villain – it was him that did it, not me.'

Fred turned the tables, claiming improbably that he had fainted and did not know the body was under the floor in the kitchen. They were both found guilty.

When asked whether they had anything to say before sentencing, Marie said: 'There is no justice and no right for a foreign subject in this country. There is no law for me. I have had no protection – neither from the judges, nor from the prosecutors, nor from my husband. I am unjustly condemned by this court.' She asserted that if she was in her own country she could have proved her innocence. After they were both sentenced to death, she yelled: 'Damnation seize ye all.'

UNFALTERING STEP

The Times of 14 November 1849 reported: 'Mrs Manning walked to her doom with a firm unfaltering step, and over her large and strongly built frame no tremor or nervous agitation of any kind was visible,' while her husband 'walked with a feeble and tottering step'.

That same day Charles Dickens who had witnessed the spectacle wrote to *The Times* saying: 'I believe that a sight so inconceivably awful as the wickedness and levity of the immense crowd collected at that execution this morning could be imagined by no man . . . The horrors of the gibbet and of the crime which brought the wretched murderers to it, faded in my mind before the atrocious bearing, looks and language, of the assembled spectators . . . screeching, and laughing, and yelling.'

Marie Manning on Patrick O'Connor

'Mr O'Connor was more to me than my husband. He was friend and brother to me ever since I came to this country. I knew him for seven years. He wanted to marry me, and I ought to have been married to him.' At one time, the two men had vied for her attention. She chose to marry Manning because he said he was expecting an inheritance. This was a lie. With his stash of railway stock O'Connor was richer – so he had to die.

HÉLÈNE JÉGADO

Arsenic Serial Killer *France, 1833–52*

After a prodigious career as a poisoner, Hélène Jégado made a big mistake. She took a job as a cook in the house of Théophile Bidard, a law professor at the University of Rennes. Even so, two of his servants were dead and another left have being debilitated by poison before Bidard eventually realized that Jégado was a killer. Only then did it become clear that she had killed many times before.

Hélène Jégado was born to a family of peasant farmers in Brittany on 28 Prairial in Year XI of the Republic, or 17 June 1803. Her mother died when she was seven years old and she was sent to live with her aunts at the presbytery in nearby Bubry where she would join them in service. At the age of eleven, she moved on with an aunt to work for the parish priest in Séglien. It was there that she seems to have begun her career as a poisoner at the age of seventeen. A girl who looked after the cows accused Hélène of putting hemp seeds in her soup. More ominously, the presbytery there was infested with rats and the parish priest sent out for some arsenic.

Jégado stayed at Séglien until she was thirty when she was sacked for 'excessive drinking'. But her elder sister Anna had just left the presbytery at Guern to go to Bubry, so Hélène replaced her at Guern as live-in cook. It was at Guern that Jégado was thought to have committed her first murder. The victim was the parish priest's sixty-six-year-old father Joseph Le Drogo, who died after a week of agony. The household were devastated, so

Father Le Drogo's sister sent his seven-year-old niece, Marie-Louise Lindevat, to the presbytery to cheer everyone up. Soon after she arrived, her grandmother, Father Le Drongo's mother, fell ill and died, followed by the child herself two weeks later.

The following month another of the servants, Marguerite André, died in agony, followed by Father Le Drogo and a second servant, Françoise Affret. Hélène's sister Anna returned for the priest's funeral and died soon after. No one suspected Hélène who had dutifully nursed all the victims. Indeed, cholera was suspected as it had killed twenty thousand in Paris the previous year.

The depleted household at Guern no longer required a cook, so Hélène replaced her dead sister at Bubry. There she nursed her aunt, Jeanne-Marie Liscouët, who soon died. The priest's sister Jeanne-Marie Lorho and his eighteen-year-old niece Jeanne-Marie Kerfontain both succumbed. Father Lorho miraculously pulled through after receiving extreme unction and his assistant, Father Jean Hervé, suffered the same symptoms with debilitating effects. Again, cholera – or possibly typhoid fever – was blamed. Again, she had to move on.

In her next household, Marie-Jeanne Leboucher and her daughter Perrine died. When eighteen-year-old son Pierre also fell ill, he refused to allow Jégado to nurse him and would eat nothing from her kitchen. He survived. A neighbour also died after drinking soup Jégado had prepared. A local doctor, Dr Pierre-Charles Toursaint, grew suspicious and found a box of powders among her things. Fearing he had overstepped the mark by searching her possessions, he put them back and failed to send them away for analysis. Then the doctor's own parents took Jégado on as a cook. His father, sister Julie and the house-keeper Anne Aveno died. Jégado herself claimed to be ill, but the doctor caught her out of bed and cooking a meal, and he sacked her. Soon after his mother also died.

By that time, Jégado had taken refuge in a nunnery. The convent then suffered a spate of mindless vandalism with clothes, bed linen and prayer books being slashed. This ceased when Jégado was caught pouring a bucket of filthy water into the harmonium, and kicked out.

Getting a job as a seamstress, she persuaded her employer, seventy-year-old Anna Le Corvec, to let her cook. The old lady died two days later. Her next employer, laundress Anne Lefur, also fell ill, but recovered when Jégado moved on. But her reputation was spreading. Dr Le Doré, the son-in-law of her next employer, threw her out, but not before she had poisoned his mother-in-law, Madame Hétel.

Jégado then found employment with the mayor of Pontivy, Pierre-François Jouanno. When his fourteen-year-old son Emile died, there was a post-mortem. His intestines were found to be inflamed. Jégado was blamed for allowing the boy to eat mustard and drink vinegar. She was sacked.

At Hennebont, Monsieur Kerally and Madame Aupy both died, but they were frail and elderly. Jégado held her next job for four years. Her employer's wife, Madame Verron, died, though this again could have been from natural causes.

In 1841, Jégado was taken on as cook at the château belonging to retired naval officer Captain Dupuy de Lôme. The family was afflicted with an epidemic of vomiting and his thirty-month-old granddaughter Marie Bréger died. After that Jégado seems to have taken a break from poisoning. This may have been because of the high-profile case of Marie Lafarge who was convicted of murdering her husband with arsenic – though she probably did not do it. Nevertheless, Jégado continued her campaign of petty theft, particularly making free with her employers' wine cellars.

The poisonings seem to have begun again in 1849 when Jégado was in Rennes, the capital of Brittany. A Madame Carrère fell ill, but recovered when her cook left. Nine-year-old Albert Rabot complained that Jégado smelt. He fell ill and died. Jégado was sacked two months later when it was noticed that wine was missing, but not before Albert's mother and grandmother had come down with an unexplained illness.

Jégado's next employer, Joseph Ozanne, also noticed wine was missing. His five-year-old son was diagnosed with croup and died within a week. She went on to work at a hotel aptly named The End of the World. The manager's mother, seventy-year-old Madame Roussel found that Jégado smelled of wine and tobacco, and decided to sack her. She fell ill. Her hands and feet were paralysed and she never recovered. Thirty-two-year-old Perrotte Macé took over as manager and died in agony. Her family refused permission for an autopsy. Jégado was then sacked after stealing a bottle of wine.

She quickly found a job at Professor Bidard's house, having been introduced by trusted chambermaid Rose Tessier. However, the new cook refused to take orders from a chambermaid half her age, but Rose stuck up for Jégado when Bidard tried to sack her. Rose soon complained of stomach pains and vomiting. Dr Pinault was called, but within three days she was dead.

When Professor Bidard started looking for a new chambermaid, Jégado objected, saying that she would take on the maid's work as well as the cooking. Nevertheless twenty-three-year-old Françoise Huriaux was employed. She, too, began to suffer from stomach pains and her hands and feet swelled up. But her mother insisted that she quit and Françoise recovered after a few weeks in hospital.

Next nineteen-year-old Rosalie Sarrazin was taken on. She fell out with Jégado when she was promoted to housekeeper because she could read and write, so Bidard gave the cook notice to quit. Bidard then became suspicious of some peas Jégado had served and refused to eat them. Instead they were given to Rosalie. After one spoonful, she was violently ill. When the doctor puzzled over the symptoms, Jégado nursed the sick girl, even preventing her mother attending the child.

Rosalie complained that soda water prescribed by the doctor

that Jégado gave her 'burnt my chest like a hot iron bar' and asked: 'What did Hélène put in it?'

Bidard questioned Jégado.

'I was struck by the expression in her eyes,' he said. 'I had never looked into her eyes before. She glanced quickly sideways at Rosalie, and her eyes were those of a wild animal, like a lion or tiger. At that moment the idea came to me that I should go into my work room, get some rope to tie her up and drag her at once before a magistrate. But I paused and reflected. I was about to brand a woman publicly on a mere suspicion. I did not know what to do. Had I before me a poisoner or a woman of admirable devotion?'

He did nothing. The doctors also kept the suspicions to themselves and soon Rosalie was dead. It was only then that he approached the Procureur de la République. He went to the house, to be greeted by Jégado. The first thing she said was: 'I am innocent.'

'Of what?' the Procureur replied. 'Nobody had accused you of anything.'

Later the police led her away. The bodies of Rose Tessier and Perrote Macé were exhumed and both contained large amounts of arsenic. The investigating magistrate was then overwhelmed with other accusations from around Brittany. However, most of them were too old to pursue. Jégado was charged with the murder of Rosalie Sarrazin, Rose Tessier and Perrote Macé, along with the attempted murder of Françoise Huriaux, Madame Rabot and a Madame Brière, and eleven counts of theft.

She denied everything. But after she was convicted, she made a confession. It does not appear to be in her own words – indeed she could not write – and was published after her death. In it, she said: 'I declare myself to be guilty of the poisonings related to the list of charges. However, I did not cause the death of my sister Anna, nor two of the other seven victims in Guern. A wicked woman was responsible for these three crimes ... It was this woman who gave me the poison I used at the start of my criminal career. It was she who encouraged me to crime and taught me how to commit it with impunity.'

On 26 February 1852, Hélèn Jégado was guillotined in front of a huge crowd on the Champ de Mars in Rennes. Her body was then handed over to the School of Medicine for experimentation.

Collecting the damning evidence

Professor Bidard gave an account of how he collected the evidence that would take Jégado to the guillotine:

> I had given order that the matter ejected by the invalid should be kept for examination. My orders had been ignored. Each time Rosalie was sick, Hélène at once emptied the vessel and cleaned it. I now took the vessels myself and locked them up in a cupboard to which I alone had the key. Jégado watched me do this with evident anxiety. From this fact I concluded that she wanted to destroy the evidence of poison administered by herself ...
>
> Rosalie suffered in the most dreadful manner. She could neither sit up nor lie down, but threw herself about with great violence. All this while, Hélène Jégado was constantly coming and going about the invalid. She lacked, however, the courage to watch her victim die ... Rosalie Sarrazin breathed her last in my presence at seven o'clock. On her return, Hélène at once looked around for the vessels containing the matter ejected by Rosalie. The ejections were green in colour. I locked them up. I sent for both Dr Pinault and Dr Baudin.
>
> After examining the vomit, they concluded that Rosalie had been poisoned and decided to report the matter.

CONSTANCE KENT

A Victorian Murder Mystery *England, 1860*

Five years after the body of three-year-old Francis 'Saville' Kent was found stuffed down a disused outhouse toilet in Road Hill House on the border of Wiltshire and Somerset, twenty-one-year-old Constance Kent admitted murdering the child. The case became a *cause célèbre* in Victorian England, inspiring murder mysteries by Charles Dickens, Wilkie Collins and Arthur Conan Doyle. Although Constance lived to be a hundred, she never recanted. However, there are some who believe that she did not do it.

Constance's father Samuel Saville Kent and his first wife Mary Ann had ten children, five of whom died young. After the birth of her tenth child, Mary Ann went insane. Samuel Kent then employed Mary Drewe Pratt as a governess and housekeeper. They became lovers and, after the death of Mary Ann, they married and had three more children; she was pregnant with her fourth child when her third, Francis, was murdered.

On the night of 29 June 1860, the child was put to bed in his nursemaid Elizabeth Gough's room. She awoke in the middle of the night to find the child missing, but thought he had been taken from his cot by his mother. However, in the morning, she discovered that this was not so. By 8 a.m., a full-scale search of the grounds was underway with Samuel Kent offering a reward of £10 – worth over £1,110 today – for the return of his son.

After about an hour, local farmer Thomas Benger and shoe-maker William Nutt pulled open the door of the servants' old toilet among the dense shrubbery in the garden. Lifting the lid, they saw what they took to be a blood-soaked blanket on the splashboard two feet below the seat. It was the body of Francis Saville Kent. When they picked him up, his head almost fell off, according to Nutt. His tongue was protruding and his mouth blackened, as if he had been suffocated.

Local superintendent John Foley suspected Elizabeth Gough, reasoning that the child could not have been taken without her knowledge. His theory was that the boy had woken up and disturbed Gough and her lover who, together, had suffocated him to keep him quiet. They had then mutilated the body to disguise the cause of death. Rumour had it that her lover was the shoemaker William Nutt, or even the boy's father, Samuel Kent himself.

Under pressure from the press, the authorities were forced to call in Scotland Yard, who despatched Detective Inspector Jonathan Whicher. Whicher dismissed Foley's theory and Elizabeth Gough was released. Instead Whicher suspected sixteen-year-old Constance and she was arrested. But when she was brought before magistrates, there was no real evidence against her and she was released. Elizabeth Gough was then charged with murder in the hope that she would implicate Samuel Kent. But she was never committed for trial.

Detective Inspector Whicher never wavered from the belief that Constance Kent murdered her brother. Outlining the case against her in twenty-three pages, he said: 'I cannot find the least motive that anyone else could have had for the act except Miss Constance . . . arising from jealousy or spite entertained towards the younger branches of the family by the second wife in consequence of the partiality shown them by the parents, and thus working on a mind somewhat affected, might have prompted her to commit the crime.'

Constance went abroad, becoming a pupil in a convent at Dinan in Brittany. When she returned three years later in 1863, she joined a religious retreat in Brighton. There she confessed her guilt to the Reverend Arthur Wagner and on 25 April 1865 – accompanied by the reverend – she walked into Bow Street Magistrate's Court and admitted murdering her stepbrother. While she spoke, she handed the Chief Magistrate Sir Thomas Henry a note which read: 'I, Constance Emile Kent, alone and unaided on the night of the 29th of June, 1860, murdered at Road Hill House, Wiltshire, one Francis Saville Kent. Before the deed none knew of my intention, nor after of my guilt; no one assisted me in the crime, nor in my evasion of discovery.' She had killed the child, she said, because he was the favourite of her stepmother who had usurped her own mother's place in the Kent household. She took great pains to clear her father's name.

Constance's confession was not universally accepted – several details of her story contradicted the facts. She said that she had murdered the child with a razor stolen from her father's wardrobe, though a wound in the boy's side had been made with a knife. Saville weighed thirty-five pounds, but Constance said she held the child – asleep and unprotesting – in one arm while she put on her galoshes, opened the window to climb out of the house, opened the privy door, lit a candle and slit the child from ear to ear. She then said that she thought the blood would never come and that the child was not killed, even though he had almost been decapitated. If the child's heart was still beating the blood would have spurted out. Even if it was not, the blood would have flowed and continued doing so for about twenty minutes. But these anomalies were not tested in court as, on 21 July, she pleaded guilty to murder at Wiltshire assizes and offered no defence. Justice Sir James Wilkes was in tears when he sentenced her to death. The sentence was commuted to penal servitude for life because of her youth at the time of the crime.

After twenty years, Constance Kent was released and went to join her brother William in Australia, living there under the name Emily Kaye. Constance died in Australia shortly after her hundredth birthday in 1944.

In her 2008 book *The Suspicions of Mr Whicher or The Murder at Road Hill House*, author Kate Summerscale concluded that Constance Kent's confession was false and she was protecting her beloved brother William, who was equally resentful of their stepmother and, at the age of fifteen, would have been strong enough to kill the child.

CATHERINE WILSON

Last Woman to Be Publicly Hanged in London
England, 1854–62

On 19 June 1862, Montagu Williams QC was in the Old Bailey awaiting the jury's verdict on a charge of attempted murder against his client, when a stranger approached him. The man congratulated Williams on his ingenious defence of forty-year-old widow Catherine Wilson, adding: 'If you succeed in getting her off, you will do her the worst turn anyone ever did her.' The stranger turned out to be a member of the Lincoln constabulary. As things stood, Wilson faced a sentence of penal servitude. When the jury returned a 'not guilty' verdict, she was immediately arrested again and charged with seven counts of wilful murder – and now faced a death sentence.

Though Catherine Wilson was only tried – and convicted – on one count of murder, she was thought to have killed as many as nine. Born in 1822, she became a nurse, but in 1850 she was working as a housekeeper for retired sea captain Peter Mawer in Boston, Lincolnshire. Suffering from rheumatism and gout, he was prescribed colchicine – a vegetable alkaloid that is fatal in overdose. Two to five hours after ingestion, the victim feels a burning sensation in the throat, followed by vomiting, fever, abdominal pain and kidney failure, causing death.

After making a will in Wilson's favour, Mawer fell ill. Two weeks later, in October 1854, he died. His death was not thought suspicious at the time and may even have been accidental. The following year, Wilson moved to London and took lodgings in a house belonging to fifty-year-old Maria Soames in Albert Street, Bloomsbury, with James Dixon, who purported to be her brother, though it was thought they were lovers. In July 1856, he died. A doctor had diagnosed rheumatic fever and Catherine Wilson had treated him with colchicine. She persuaded the doctor not to conduct a post-mortem, saying Dixon had a morbid fear of being cut up.

Soon after, Mrs Soames came home one evening, after borrowing £9 from her brother. She was in good health. Mrs Wilson asked to talk to her privately. The following morning Mrs Soames fell violently ill. A doctor was called and Mrs Wilson volunteered to nurse her landlady, feeding her and giving her medicine. When she died, the £9 could not be found. Mrs Wilson had produced an IOU for £10 from Mrs Soames, which later proved to be forged. She also spread the rumour that Mrs Soames had taken poison because a man had jilted her. The man was never found, though a letter arrived from him – also later found to be in Mrs Wilson's handwriting.

In 1859, Mrs Wilson returned to Boston, where she worked for a Mrs Jackson. Then, four days after Mrs Jackson withdrew £120 from the bank, she died; the money had gone missing.

Back in London, Mrs Wilson could now afford a house in Lambeth, large enough to take in lodgers. One of them was fifty-five-year-old Ann Atkinson, who ran a millinery shop in Kirby Lonsdale in Cumberland (now Cumbria). She had come to London with a large sum of money to buy stock for the shop.

Soon, her husband received a telegram, informing him that his wife was gravely ill. By the time he reached London, she was already dead. Mrs Wilson told him that his wife had implored her not to let anyone cut up her body, so Mr Atkinson refused permission for an autopsy. He also wondered where the money she had been carrying was. Mrs Wilson feigned surprise that Mrs Atkinson had not written to her husband to inform him that on the train to London, she had felt unwell. Getting off at Rugby, she had been resting in the waiting room when the money had been stolen. Mrs Wilson was wearing the dead woman's diamond ring, which she said Mrs Atkinson had given to her for safe keeping.

In February 1862, Mrs Wilson nursed Sarah Carnell, a frail and elderly woman who lived in Marylebone. In gratitude, Mrs Carnell promised her a large legacy. It seems that Mrs Wilson had run out of colchicine. But Catherine Wilson eventually volunteered to get some fresh medicine, returning with what she described as a soothing draught.

Mrs Carnell said that she felt the liquid was hot through the bottom of the glass, but Mrs Wilson said: 'Drink it down, love; it will warm you.' When Mrs Carnell took a mouthful, it was so hot that she spat it out on the bedclothes. The liquid burnt holes in the counterpane – it turned out to be sulphuric acid. Catherine Wilson fled, but was captured a couple of days later and stood trial in the Old Bailey.

The ingenious defence put up by Catherine Wilson's lawyer, Montagu Williams, was that, when Mrs Wilson went to fetch the medicine, the doctor was out and the fifteen-year-old lad temporarily in charge of the dispensary had given her the wrong medicine. In his summing up, the judge said this defence was untenable: had the acid been in the bottle as Mrs Wilson received it at the time, rather than a special container, it would have become red hot or burst before she got home. Nevertheless, to everyone's surprise, the jury acquitted her. Mrs Wilson was delighted. But as she turned to leave the dock she was re-arrested.

Mrs Soames's, daughter had recognized Mrs Wilson as the woman who had been nursing her mother when she died and the authorities had begun looking into her background. The bodies of her other victims were disinterred and traces of poison were found. However, in court, Montagu Williams maintained that it was impossible to detect a poison such as colchicine after even a short time had elapsed. In his summing up, the judge also dismissed this line of defence.

'Gentlemen, if such a state of things as this were allowed to exist,' he said, 'no living person could sit down to a meal in safety.'

He then sent the jury out for lunch. They returned a verdict of guilty and, as Mrs Wilson was sentenced to death, the other indictments – six counts of murder – were not proceeded with.

At 8 a.m. on Monday, 20 October 1862, a crowd of between twenty and thirty thousand packed the streets around the Old Bailey to witness the hanging. It was the first execution of a woman in fourteen years. On the gallows, Catherine Wilson was asked if she had anything to say. She replied: 'I am innocent.'

LYDIA SHERMAN

The Derby Poisoner *USA, 1867–71*

Horatio N. Sherman, a widower with four children, had good reason to turn to drink. Soon after marrying Lydia Danbury, two of his children had died. Then, after a week-long drinking spree, Horatio himself fell ill and died. His doctor was suspicious. He obtained permission to conduct a post-mortem and sent the deceased's liver to the professor of toxicology at Yale, who found it was saturated with arsenic. Lydia Sherman was arrested. It was then discovered that she had also poisoned her previous two husbands and seven of her children.

L ydia Danbury was born in Burlington, New Jersey in 1825. Orphaned at the age of just nine months, she was brought up by an uncle. At church, the sixteen-year-old met Edward Struck, a forty-year-old widower with four children. They married and, together, they had a further six children.

The family had moved to Manhattan where Struck took a job as a policeman. However, in 1863, he was sacked for failing to respond quickly enough to prevent the murder of a detective in a bar-room brawl. The dismissal seemed to have left him unhinged. Lydia decided that he was no further use to her and despatched him by putting arsenic in his porridge. The death certificate said he died of 'consumption'.

Lydia was then a forty-two-year-old widow with no income. Struck's children from his first marriage had already grown up and left home, and one of them died of an undiagnosed intestinal ailment. But she still had five mouths to feed. The first to go were the youngest – four-year-old Edward and six-year-old Martha Ann. Again she used arsenic. The doctor diagnosed gastric fever.

Next her fourteen-year-old son who was working as a decorator came down with 'painter's colic' – poisoning cause by toxic lead pigments. As he could no longer earn money for the family he had to go with a little arsenic in his tea. Cause of death: painter's colic.

Twelve-year-old Ann Eliza had always been frail. When she came down with fever in March 1866, a few grains of arsenic in her medication finished her off. Cause of death: typhoid fever. Then in May, Lydia Sherman's last surviving child, eighteen-year-old Lydia, was struck down with fever. She dutifully took the foul-tasting medicine her mother gave her, had convulsions and died.

The poisoner now only had herself to look after. She took a job in Stratford, Connecticut, as housekeeper to a wealthy farmer named Dennis Hurlburt. They married, but the following year he became ill after eating a bowl of his wife's special clam chowder. His death was attributed to cholera. He left her $10,000 and a house.

Then she applied to become a housekeeper for Horatio Sherman, a wealthy widower with four children living in Derby, Connecticut. She was quite taken with Sherman when she met him, but after they married she discovered that he was an alcoholic who could not be trusted with money, and she began to fear for her Hurlburt inheritance. Another problem was Sherman's mother-in-law who stayed on to nurse the youngest child, four-month-old Frankie. Lydia solved the problem by putting arsenic in his milk. Next, she poisoned fourteen-year-old Ada.

Lydia encouraged her husband to join a temperance society and he kept the pledge for several weeks, but then sold the piano for $300 and went on a binge. Before dying he complained of having 'one of my old spells', but his doctor did not think his symptoms were consistent with any alcohol-related illness and suspected foul play.

By the time the test results had come back from Yale, Lydia Sherman had returned to New York City. She was arrested there and shipped back to Connecticut. Meanwhile the bodies of Frankie, Ada and Hurlburt had been exhumed and were found to contain arsenic. However, she was charged only with the murder of Sherman and stood trial in New Haven, Connecticut, in March 1872. The defence argued that Sherman had taken his own life over his financial difficulties and the loss of two of his children, but the jury found Lydia guilty only of second-degree murder on the grounds that the circumstantial nature of the evidence permitted 'reasonable doubt' and she was sentenced to life imprisonment. If she had been a man – or in any other state but Connecticut – she would have hanged.

In December 1872, she began making her confession to her jailer, Captain Webster, as she could barely write. She admitted poisoning Struck, the children and Hurlburt. She also admitted buying arsenic in New Haven, but did not intend to kill Sherman – only some household rats and the children. However, she said that Sherman liked to put saleratus, or bicarbonate of soda, in his cider to make it foam. The arsenic and the saleratus got mixed up. She even claimed to have drunk some of it herself, but recovered. However, she admitted that she did not warn him of the danger.

'It is curious that the only death for which she could not be held accountable, according to her story, should be that for which she has been convicted,' remarked the *Hartford Courant*.

The confession was not used against her as she was not prosecuted for the other murders. She was confined in the state prison in Wethersfield, Connecticut, but managed to escape. Recaptured, her health broke down and she died in 1878, aged fifty-three.

The song of Lydia Sherman

In an era where Lizzie Borden, who was acquitted of the axe-murder of her parents, got a ditty written about her, The Derby

Poisoner – aka The Poison Fiend, The Queen Poisoner and The Borgia of Connecticut – certainly deserved one after her sensational trial.

> Lydia Sherman is plagued with rats
> Lydia has no faith in cats.
> So Lydia buys some arsenic,
> And then her husband, he gets sick;
> And then her husband, he does die,
> And Lydia's neighbours wonder why.
> Lydia moves, but still has rats;
> And still she puts no faith in cats;
> So again she buys some arsenic.
> This time her children; they get sick,
> This time her children, they do die,
> And Lydia's neighbours wonder why.
> Lydia lies in Wethersfield jail,
> And loudly does she moan and wail.
> She blames her fate on a plague of rats;
> She blames the laziness of cats.
> But her neighbours' questions, she can't deny –
> So Lydia now in prison must lie.

MARY ANN COTTON

The Dark Angel *England, 1852–72*

Asked by a parish official about her domestic arrangements after she married her latest paramour Mr Quick-Manning, Mary Ann Cotton said of her stepson: 'The boy's in the way. Perhaps it won't matter as I won't be troubled long. He'll go like all the rest of the Cotton family.' A week later he was dead. However, the doctor refused to issue a death certificate, so the insurance company withheld his burial money. An inquest found that the child had died of natural causes. However, local newspapers noted that, as a comparatively young woman, she had already been through three husbands – in a time when a divorce was difficult to obtain. Her children also showed an alarming mortality rate and rumours circulated that she was a poisoner.

At the age of twenty, Mary Ann Robson married collier William Mowbray. They moved around the country, having nine children – five of whom died along the way. The couple took the remaining children to Sunderland, where Mary Ann became a nurse. This gave her access to drugs and poisons.

Mowbray died in 1865. His death certificate said he died of typhus fever. British Prudential paid out £35 on his life insurance, which would be worth over £4,000 in today's money. Two more of their children died soon after.

Mary Ann then moved to Seaham Harbour, south of Sunderland, to be with her lover Joseph Nattrass, a married man. Another child died. After a couple of months, Mary Ann returned to Sunderland where she worked in the infirmary, while her remaining child was sent to live with her mother.

At the hospital she met her second husband, George Ward, who was described on their marriage certificate as an engineer – that is, he tended the engine on a steam tug. Although described as a 'well-built and normally strong man', he died at the age of thirty-three just fourteen months after their wedding. The cause of death was given as 'English cholera and typhoid fever', though his symptoms were consistent with arsenic poisoning. He was buried the next day with no post-mortem and the Prudential paid out again.

Mary Ann then became housekeeper to widower James Robinson and his five children. Almost immediately, his five-year-old son died. Soon after she fell pregnant. She then went to nurse her mother, who was ill. She died nine days after Mary Ann arrived. The death certificate said hepatitis though, again, the symptoms were consistent with arsenic poisoning. Mary Ann's remaining child died soon after she returned with her to Robinson's house, followed quickly by Robinson's eldest daughter.

The couple were married in August 1867. Their first child, a daughter, was born in November. She was dead the following February. In June 1869, Mary Ann had a son, George, who survived her. Robinson had refused to take out life insurance on himself or his children. This probably saved their lives. He then discovered that Mary Ann had been running up debts and was stealing from his bank account. His son also said that his stepmother sent him out to pawn clothes and household items. When Robinson discovered this, he kicked his wife out. Mary Ann took baby George with her, but she left him with a friend, saying she was going to post a letter. She never returned.

Mary Ann was then introduced to Frederick Cotton by his sister Margaret. After his wife and two daughters died, Mary Ann took over as housekeeper to look after his two sons. Margaret died in March 1870 from 'pleuropneumia' after suffering severe stomach pains and leaving £60 to her brother. The following month Mary Ann was pregnant.

That September, Frederick and Mary Ann were married and she was quick to have him take out life insurance on his sons Frederick Jr and Charles Edward. Their own son Robert Robson Cotton was born early the next year. The family then moved to West Auckland, near Joseph Nattrass.

Frederick Cotton died in September 1871 of 'typhoid and hepatitis', aged forty. Three months later Nattrass moved in. Mary Ann advertised her services as a nurse and was taken on by an excise officer named Quick-Manning who was recovering from smallpox. In March 1872, Frederick Jr died of 'gastric fever', Robert Robson of 'convulsions from teething' and Nattrass of 'typhoid fever'. She did not have her baby buried until Nattrass died too, saving money by having them buried together. It seems she was already pregnant with Quick-Manning's baby.

Quick-Manning objected when Mary Ann took in a male lodger, so she took money from the parish to support Charles Edward. She asked the parish official Thomas Riley to put Charles Edward in the Bishop Auckland Workhouse. When he refused, she said that he would not be in the way very long.

'You don't mean to tell me that this little healthy fellow is going to die?' said Riley.

'He'll not get up,' said Mary Ann. Riley took this to mean that he would not reach manhood.

When the child died, Riley reported the conversation to the police and Dr William Kilburn who attended the boy. Dr Kilburn did not have enough time to conduct a thorough post-mortem and, at the inquest, suggested that the boy had died from gastroenteritis. The jury returned the verdict of death by natural causes. Suspicions that Charles Edward had been murdered by his stepmother did not die down. Four days after the inquest, Dr Kilburn performed tests on the contents of the child's stomach, which he had kept back, and discovered arsenic.

Mary Ann Cotton was arrested and charged with the murders of Charles Edward, Nattrass, Frederick Cotton Jr and Robert Robson Cotton, but the trial was delayed until after she had given birth to Quick-Manning's child, one of the two of Cotton's thirteen to survive their mother. Her defence was that no one had seen her administer the poison. The jury returned a verdict of guilty. Petitions for clemency fell on deaf ears and she was hanged in Durham County, using the old-fashioned long-drop method. Instead of breaking the neck causing death instantaneously, this slowly strangled, making her death slow and painful.

Testimony of Jane Hedley

I lived at West Auckland and was very friendly with the prisoner. I assisted her about her house backwards and forwards. I assisted during the time of illness of Joseph Nattrass. I saw him several times during his illness. The prisoner waited on him and was constantly about him. I saw no one else wait on him. The prisoner gave him anything he required. Nattrass was several times sick and purged. This [sic] was occasionally he complained of pain at the bottom of his bowels. I saw him have fits, he was twisted up and seemed in great agony. He twisted his toes and his hand and worked them all ways. He drew his legs quite up. He was throwing himself about a good deal and the prisoner held him and had to use great force. He was unconscious when in the fits. After the fits were over he sometimes said it was a very strong one and sometimes said it was not. Robert Robson Cotton died on the Thursday before Easter and was laid out in the same room where Nattrass was.

On the Friday before Nattrass died I was in the prisoner's house with Dr Richardson, Nattrass and the prisoner. Dr Richardson asked him if the pain had left him. He said no. Dr Richardson then said if he could stop the purging he thought he would get better. Nattrass said it is no fever I have. The doctor said if he knew better than him it was no use his coming. He then asked Nattrass if he had taken the medicine and he said no. I was present just at the time of Nattrass's death. He died in a fit, which was similar to the previous ones. The prisoner was holding him down. I did not say anything about Nattrass having proper support. I have seen her several times give him a drink.

On the Thursday before Nattrass died the prisoner told me that Nattrass had said she, the prisoner, was to have his watch and club money, as she had been his best friend. On the same day the prisoner asked me to get a letter written for the burial money from the club of the deceased. I lived about half a dozen houses from the prisoner at this time. Shortly after Nattrass's death, namely about a week, the prisoner was in my house assisting to clean. She sent me to her house for a pot that stood on the pantry shelf. She said there was soft soap and arsenic in this pot. I went for and got this pot and showed it to the prisoner. She said it was the right one and what she got to clean beds with . . .

MARTHA NEEDLE

Black Widow of Richmond *Australia, 1885–94*

Martha Needle murdered her husband and three children, gaining an insurance payout of £300, which would be worth over £35,000 now. Intent on marrying again, she went on to murder her would-be husband's brother who was against the match, only to be arrested while trying to kill a second brother. Even so, her intended stuck by her, saying: 'She didn't know what she was doing.' She too insisted on her innocence to the end. Nevertheless, she accepted her fate and went unprotesting to the gallows.

Born Martha Charles in 1863 on the Murray River near Morgan, South Australia, Martha was brought up in a household torn by domestic violence. Fortunately, her father died when she was young. At twelve she went into domestic service in Port Adelaide, where she met and married Henry Needle, a carpenter six years her senior. They had three children and moved to Melbourne.

By then the marriage did not seem to be a happy one. Needle was jealous and Martha regularly went out without him. In 1885, their daughter, three-year-old Mabel, fell ill and died. Martha collected an insurance payout of £100 sterling.

Around that time Henry Needle went to Sydney, looking for work. After he returned, he too fell ill. He was not a good patient and refused the food and drink provided by his wife, though he died without saying why. The cause of death was given as 'subacute hepatitis, enteric fever, and exhaustion due to obstinacy in not taking nourishment'. Although he had done himself no favours starving himself, there were symptoms of inflammation of the liver and intestine consistent with having been poisoned. This time the insurance company were to pay out £200, but Martha only received £60 – a third of the sum, minus expenses. The rest was to be invested by the company for the benefit of the two remaining children.

The following year, five-year-old Elsie died of 'gangrenous stomatitis and exhaustion' after an illness of three weeks. Martha got her share, another £60. The year after that, two-year-old May died from 'tubercular meningitis'.

At the beginning of 1892, Martha became housekeeper to Otto and Louis Junckens, saddlers in Richmond. Within a few months, she was engaged to Otto. Louis objected because of Martha's filthy temper. His mother also wrote, opposing the marriage.

Louis soon fell ill, but on his sickbed he had a change of heart and was reprieved. There seems to have been difficulties the following year, when he was again seized with bouts of violent vomiting. When a relative came to look after him, he got better again. But when they went, Martha went out and bought a box of rodent poison called Rough on Rats. The next day, Martha made Louis his breakfast. He died five days later. The cause of death was said to be exhaustion and inflammation of the stomach and membranes of the heart possibly caused by typhoid.

Then Otto and Louis's mother arrived with brother Hermann. As he backed his mother's objections to the marriage, Hermann was next on Martha's death list. After eating a meal prepared by Martha, he fell ill. He recovered, but fell ill again the following day after breakfast. Two days later he was seized with violent stomach cramps after eating lunch, again prepared by Martha.

The physician who attended him, Dr Boyd, suspect poison. Samples of Hermann's vomit were tested and arsenic was found. Dr Boyd went to the police who aimed to set a trap. They waited outside. When Martha served Hermann a cup of tea, he blew a whistle and police came bursting in, in time to prevent Martha knocking over the cup. It contained ten grains of arsenic, enough to kill five people.

Initially Martha was arrested for attempted murder. The body of Louis Juncken was then disinterred and found to contain thirty-four grains of arsenic. Henry Needle, Mabel, Elsie and May were also exhumed. Only May's body was found to contain arsenic. The others had been dead and buried too long to permit analysis.

Martha was charged with the murder of Louis Juncken. She pleaded not guilty. The trial took three days. The jury then took forty minutes to return a guilty verdict and Supreme Court Justice Hodge gave her a sentence of death.

One newspaper reported: 'The prisoner received the death sentence with extraordinary calmness. She walked out of the dock unassisted, with a firm step and unblanched face.'

In prison, it was said: 'None of those who are thrown into contact with Martha Needle can fathom her character. The condemned woman's mask of impenetrable reserve has confessedly baffled the governor of the gaol. Dr Shields, the Government medical officer, and both her spiritual advisers (Mr H.F. Scott, Church of England chaplain, and Mrs Hutchinson, of the Salvation Army). Even to these experienced eyes the extraordinary woman is as inscrutable as the Sphinx. No hope of a reprieve has been expressed by her at any time, in fact she has firmly stated that she prefers death.'

She was equally taciturn on the gallows. Despite her insistence on her innocence, asked for her last words, she said: 'I have nothing to say.'

She was hanged at 8 a.m. on 22 October 1894. By then she had spent most of the insurance money she had received on an elaborate family grave, which she had visited regularly. In her will she bequeathed whatever was left to Otto. This amounted to a £25 life insurance policy.

Martha Needle's last letter

A few hours before she was executed, Martha wrote to Otto, saying:

Melbourne Gaol, Monday, 4 o'clock.

My Darling – As you wished me to write I will do so, but truly I do not know what to say to you on this my last morning on earth. In a few hours I shall be free from all sorrow, but you, dear Otto, must live on for a time. It may be a very long time or it may not, but whichever way God wishes it will be. But, never mind try to bear up under the very sad blow. Rest assured we shall meet again where there is no parting. Your good father, also poor Louis and my dear little ones will welcome you. You know, dear, Elsie and May loved you on earth they will do so in heaven. Think how they will all welcome you to our happy home on high. I must ask you not to think unkindly of me for saying what I did last night to Mr Scott. I think it right that you should know what that man did say about you but I want you to thoroughly understand that I did not believe that you ever did say so to him, and I told him so. You must not think what he said upset me, for it did not, only it annoyed me to think that such a man would tell an untruth. True, he may think he was doing right we must hope he did think so. Now you will want to know what sort of a night I have had – fairly good. You and all dear ones have been in my thoughts and prayers, dear Otto. Please read the 139th Psalm from the 7th to the 13th verse, as I have asked God to forgive me anything that I have done to displease Him, and trust to His forgiveness, so do I forgive all that have ever done me any sort of unkindness, for I know that they are very sorry now for me, be the wrong little or big. Give my everlasting love to all enquiring friends. I must now say good-bye to you for a time. When you receive this you can think of me as being in a happy home with my loved ones waiting and watching for you. I know, dear Otto that you will get ready for that happy meeting with us all. With love and sympathy from your loving Martha.

Two hours later she included in the envelope verses from a hymn that begins: 'Farewell, faithful ones, I must now bid adieu to the joys and the pleasures I've tasted with you.' These were also addressed to Otto. She also added a short prayer, beginning: 'This will be my last prayer in thought.'

Two hours after that, she was hanged.

AMELIA DYER

The Reading Baby Farmer *England, 1869–96*

Also known as the Ogress of Reading, Amelia Dyer was convicted of murdering two children. For over thirty years, she had been in the business of baby farming – that is, the Victorian practice of taking in unwanted children for a fee then, in some cases, murdering them. The bodies of seven known victims were found in the River Thames at Reading – 'You'll know mine by the tape around their necks,' she said. But the body count may have been as much as three or four hundred, making her one of the most prolific serial killers in history.

On 30 March 1896, a bargeman spotted a brown paper parcel floating in the Thames near the mouth of the River Kennet at Reading. When he caught hold of it with his punt-hook, the wet paper tore and a baby's leg stuck out. He hauled the parcel on board the barge and found that it contained the naked body of a baby girl wrapped in sheets of paper. At the police station, it was found that the very last sheet of paper, the one closest to the body, had a label from Bristol Temple Meads Station and a name and address: 'Mrs Thomas, 26 Piggott's Road, Lower Caversham.' The police went to that address and discovered that Mrs Thomas had moved. It took five days to discover that she was then living under the name Mrs Harding at 45 Kensington Road, Reading.

Meanwhile an advertisement had appeared in the *Bristol Times & Mirror*. It read: 'NURSE CHILD – Wanted, respectable woman to take young child at home – State terms to Mrs Scott,

23 Manchester Street, Cheltenham.' Alongside it in the Miscellaneous Wants column was another small ad that read: 'MARRIED couple with no family would adopt healthy child, nice country home. Terms, £10 – Harding, care of Ship's Letter Exchange, Stokes Croft, Bristol.'

Mrs Scott was, in fact, twenty-three-year-old barmaid Evelina Edith Marmon, who was unmarried and was not in a position to support her three-month-old baby daughter Doris. She was looking for someone to take care of her child for a weekly fee in the hope that, if her circumstances changed, she could reclaim her later.

Evelina exchanged letters with Mrs Harding, who assured her: 'Myself and my husband are dearly fond of children. I have no child of my own. A child with me will have a good home and a mother's love and care. We belong to the Church of England.' In fact, Mrs Dyer, alias Harding, had long separated from her husband and had two children – a son and a daughter – of her own.

The day after the body of the baby girl had been fished from the Thames, Mrs Dyer went to Cheltenham to collect Doris. From there, Dyer took Doris on the train to Paddington. They then took the bus to Mayo Road, Willesden, where Mrs Dyer's daughter Mary Ann – known as Polly – lived with her husband Alfred Palmer. It was in their home that Dyer strangled Doris.

The next day, Mrs Dyer and Polly, with another child she had adopted for £12, went to Paddington Station to collect thirteen-month-old Harry Simmons. They returned to Polly's home in Mayo Road. When Harry began to cry, Mrs Dyer strangled him too.

That evening she went with her daughter and son-in-law to see the Sporting and Military Show at Olympia. The Palmers slept soundly that night. Mrs Dyer settled down again on the couch. In the early hours, she was awoken by what she thought was the sound of a baby crying. Checking under the couch she found the two little bundles containing the dead children there quite still.

The following afternoon, Mrs Dyer packed the two little bundles into a carpet bag, adding two bricks from next door's garden. Polly and Arthur then accompanied her to Paddington, where she caught the 9.15 p.m. train to Reading. She ate a pastry she had bought on the way. It was a fast train, arriving in Reading at 10.05 p.m. It was raining as she lugged the heavy bag down the dark streets to the river. After she made sure there was nobody about, she pushed the bag through the railings of the Clappers footbridge. It made a loud splash as it hit the water. As she hurried home, she was spotted by John Toller, an engineer from Reading Gaol. He saw that she was empty handed.

The police made enquiries and discovered that Mrs Harding was in the business of adopting children. They sent a young woman to 45 Kensington Road. Mrs Harding was not there, but she was greeted by an old lady of about seventy who identified herself as 'Granny Smith'. The young woman made an appointment to see Mrs Harding two days later. When she returned then, Mrs Harding agreed to adopt a child, which the young woman should bring 'tomorrow evening after dark'. Instead Detective Constable James Anderson and Sergeant Harry James turned up at the front door.

Mrs Harding appeared visibly shocked. Under questioning she revealed that her real name was Dyer, though she sometimes used the name Thomas, which was the surname of her first husband. She could offer no explanation of how the paper bearing her former address had been used to wrap the child's body found in the Thames, saying only that she had received a package when she was living at Caversham and had put the wrapping paper in the bin with the rest of the rubbish.

The officers searched the house and found piles of baby wear and pawn tickets for children's clothing. There were also a number of vaccination certificates and correspondence concerning the adoption of children for money. The stench coming from the cupboard under the stairs indicated that a body had been left decomposing there before it had been disposed of. In a sewing basket, the police found white tape, similar to that found around the neck of the child fished from the Thames.

Dyer was arrested and taken to the police station. While she waited for a woman to arrive to search her, she produced a small pair of scissors, which had to be wrested from her. She then tried to hang herself with her bootlace.

After discovering the effects of other children in Dyer's home, the police began dragging the river. The bodies of seven children were found in all, but only two could be identified. Dyer was charged with the murder of Doris Marmon and Harry Simmons. The police also visited Mayo Road. Arthur Palmer was charged as an accomplice and there was a strong suspicion that Polly must also have known of her mother's activities. However, Dyer made a confession from Reading Gaol, exonerating them.

Dyer was associated with the deaths of other children in her care. After leaving her husband, she moved often and changed her name frequently so concerned parents could not discover the fate of their offspring. When a doctor became suspicious over the number of deaths he was being asked to certify, Dyer received six months' hard labour for causing death by neglect. After that, she spent spells in mental hospitals and the workhouse. During one of them she met Granny Smith, a naïf who unwittingly became her accomplice.

At the Old Bailey, Dyer confessed to the killings, but pleaded insanity. It took the jury less than five minutes to return a guilty verdict. She was hanged at Newgate Prison on 10 June 1896. The case gave a boost to the newly formed National Society for the Prevention of Cruelty to Children and the laws concerning adoption were tightened.

Two years after Dyer's execution, a three-week-old girl was

found wrapped in a parcel under a seat of a railway carriage in a siding in Newton Abbot. The child was alive and had recently been adopted by a 'Mrs Stewart'. When she was arrested, she turned out to be Dyer's daughter Polly.

ADA CHARD WILLIAMS

Hanged for a Knot *England, 1899*

Another of the notorious Victorian baby farmers was Ada Chard Williams. Although she was convicted of the murder of just one child, she admitted that others died in her care. Her husband, who shared the dock of the Old Bailey with her, was acquitted of murder. He was also acquitted of assisting and harbouring his wife when the prosecution offered no evidence. Ada was sentenced to death and became the last woman to be hanged in Newgate Prison.

On 17 December 1897, Florence Jones, an unmarried serving girl, gave birth to a daughter, whom she named Selina Ellen Jones. Unable to look after the child, she paid Mrs Martha Wetherall five shillings a week to care for her. Florence visited the child but could not continue the arrangement when the father stopped making any contribution.

She then saw an advertisement in the *Woolwich Herald* that said: 'ADOPTION – A young married couple would adopt healthy baby; every care and comfort; good references given; very small premium. Write first to Mrs Hewetson, 4, Bradmore Lane, Hammersmith.'

She wrote and arranged to meet Mrs Hewetson and agreed to pay her £5. She would visit her daughter once a fortnight, she said, and would take her back when her circumstances improved. On 31 August 1899, the day Florence brought over Selina and her clothes, she only had £3 and said she would pay the remaining £2 on the following Sunday. Mrs Hewetson then took her to a house in the Grove, Hammersmith, which was where she said she was going to live with the child. But they could not go in as workmen were currently refurbishing. Instead they went on to see a Mrs Woolmer, at 2 Southerton Road, where Mrs Hewetson introduced Florence as her sister-in-law.

When they parted Mrs Hewetson said that she would send a letter, telling Florence where the £2 was to be delivered. None came. She went to 4 Bradmore Lane to find that it was a news-agent's people used as a mail drop. The people who had then moved into the house in the Grove knew nothing of a Mrs Hewetson and Mrs Woolmer was merely a landlady who had rented Mrs Hewetson a room for 'me and my baby' for the night, though she disappeared soon after Florence had left. Florence then went to the police station to make a complaint.

The police soon discovered that Mrs Hewetson had moved to 3 Grove Villas, Grove Road in Barnes, though she had already disappeared in the night without paying the rent. Neighbours said they knew her as Mrs Chard Williams, who was twenty-four. She had lived there with her forty-seven-year-old husband William, who had an MA from Cambridge and was a tutor at a college in Clapham. They had with them two adopted children – ten-month-old Freddy and Lily, who answered to the description of Selina Jones, then twenty months old.

Mrs Dagmar Loughborough, who lived next door, said she saw Mrs Williams smack Lily. On another occasion, when she was crying, Mrs Loughborough heard Mr Williams say to Mrs Williams: 'Don't do that.'

Mrs Williams replied: 'You mind your own damned business, or I will serve you the same.' She then came out into the garden and told Mrs Loughborough that Lily had 'dirtied on the floor, and she had beaten her with a stick for doing so, and left her lying in it, and Mr Williams had taken the child up to the bath-room and changed its linen ... and that he had taken the stick from her.'

Mrs Loughborough said: 'Poor little thing!' Mrs Williams replied: 'Serve it right.'

A day or two later Mrs Loughborough went into Number 3 again, and Mrs Williams showed her some weals on the child's back.

'They stood out as thick as my finger,' she said. The marks were dark red.

Mrs Williams said: 'Look what I have done.'

'What would the mother say if she saw them?' said Mrs Loughborough.

'I don't care what the mother would say,' said Mrs Williams.

Lily was painfully thin and cried continually, but one day after visiting relatives in Greenwich Mrs Loughborough returned to find her neighbours' house quiet.

'How unusually quiet Lily is!' she said to Mrs Williams the following day. Williams said that the child's mother had come and taken her home.

'It is a damned good job it has gone; now I feel in Heaven,' she said.

She also told Mrs Loughborough that Lily's mother had left some of the child's clothes behind and was willing to exchange them for a decorated flower pot she had seen in her house.

On 27 September 1899, the body of a child wrapped in a brown paper parcel was washed up on the bank of the Thames at Battersea. It was identified to be that of Selina Ellen Jones. She had been in the water for about four days and had been battered and strangled.

After she had disappeared from Barnes, Mrs Williams wrote to the police, saying that she had passed the child on to a Mrs Smith in Croydon. Eventually the fugitive couple were arrested in Hackney in December. They still had Freddy with them. They were charged with the murder of Selina Ellen Jones, aka Lily, and appeared at the Old Bailey on 16 February 1900. Ada Williams turned a chair towards the jury, gazing appealingly at them. William, on the other hand, looked downtrodden, though he still looked tenderly at his wife.

Evidence was presented that William had opposed his wife's baby-farming and had treated the children kindly. The police surgeon said that the child whose body had been found had been stunned with a blow to the head before being strangled with a string around her neck.

The damning piece of evidence was a special 'fisherman's knot' used to tie up the brown paper package containing the child's body. A similar knot was found in a sash-cord at 3 Grove Villas.

When Ada Chard Williams was sentenced to death, she screamed and hit out at the wardress. Although acquitted on the murder charges, William Chard Williams did not walk free. He was immediately re-arrested on a charge of fraud.

The letter

To the Secretary, Criminal Investigation Department, New Scotland Yard, W.

Sir, I must apologise taking this liberty, but I see by the papers that I, in conjunction with my husband, are suspected of murdering the little female child found at Battersea on September 27th. The accusation is positively false. The facts of the case are these: I, much against my husband's wish, in August last advertised for a child, thinking to make a little money, the result of which was the adoption of this little child, with whom I received the sum £3. My next act was to advertise for a home for a little girl; I used some shop in Warwick Road, West Kensington, I forget the number, but I used the name of Denton, or Dalton, I am not sure which. I received about 40 replies, from which I chose one, from George Street or George Road, Croydon. The lady from Croydon, Mrs Smith by name, agreed to take the child for £1 and clothes. I met her at Clapham Junction, the Falcon Hotel, on a Saturday about the middle of September; we were to meet at 7 o'clock. I arrived at time, but Mrs Smith was

20 minutes late. I handed the child over to her, and she was then quite well. That is the last I saw of her. I have, it is true, been carrying on a sort of baby-farm; that is to say, I have adopted babies, and then advertised and got them re-adopted for about half the amount I had previously received. I have had five in this way; two died while in my care, but I can prove that every attention and kindness was shown them; no money was grudged over their illness. I can prove this by the people with whom we lodged, and also by the doctors who attended them. Two I have had re-adopted; one went to Essex, the other to Bristol, and the last one I parted with as above stated. From the accounts in the papers I am alleged to have carried on this system for six years; now, that, too, is utterly wrong. I am evidently mistaken for someone else, as the first one I ever adopted was in November, 1897. You will say, 'If innocent, why not come forward?' There have been innocent people hanged before now, and I must admit that at the present things look very much against me, but it is not fair to go entirely on circumstantial evidence. I am trying to find the woman to whom I gave up the child, but, unfortunately for me, I destroyed her letters, and if I came forward there would be no possibility of clearing myself unless I could find some clue about her. In conclusion, I must tell you that my husband is not to blame in any way whatever; he has always looked upon the whole matter with the greatest abhorrence, but only gave way to me because he was, through illness, out of employment; he never, however, once touched any of the money I made by these means.

Yours truly,
M. HEWETSON.

P.S. – We left Barnes simply because we were unable to meet the rent, and some time before we heard of this lamentable affair. The shop in Warwick Road is a newspaper shop, the Hammersmith Road end, and only a few doors down on the right-hand side.

JANE TOPPAN

Jolly Jane *USA, 1880–1901*

The poisoner Jane Toppan said she wanted 'to be known as the greatest criminal who ever lived'. In jail awaiting trial, she told newspapermen that she had given the consultant psychiatrist and the attorney general 'the names of thirty-one persons I killed, but, as a matter of fact, I killed many more whose names I cannot recall. I think it would be safe to say I killed at least a hundred from the time I became a nurse at Boston hospital, where I killed the first one.' However, she was not considered a criminal at all. She was acquitted of murder on the grounds of inherited insanity.

Born Nora Kelley in Boston in 1854, she lost her mother when an infant and her abusive alcoholic father went insane. A sister later followed him to the asylum. Their grandmother was unable to look after the children, so Nora was sent to an orphanage. There, at the age of five, she was adopted by Abner and Ann Toppan, who changed her name to Jane and took her to live in Lowell, Massachusetts.

Jane did well at school, though it was her foster sister who was sought after by the boys in Lowell. Nevertheless, Jane got engaged, but when her fiancé went to find work seventy miles away in Holyoke he married his landlady's daughter there. Jane hammered her engagement ring to pieces. She then became withdrawn and twice tried to kill herself.

At the age of twenty-six, she decided to study nursing at a hospital in Cambridge, Massachusetts, where she was hardworking and popular – and known as 'Jolly Jane' – though she showed a ghoulish interest in autopsies. When two patients under her care died mysteriously, she was fired. These early killings she considered 'practice murders'. She later admitted getting a sexual thrill from watching victims as they lost consciousness and would cradle them as they died. One patient who survived the bitter-tasting medicine Toppan had given her said she climbed into bed with her and began kissing her all over the face.

Jane went on to work at Massachusetts General Hospital, Boston, where she continued killing patients. Her method was to use a mixture of morphine and atrophine, the active ingredient in belladonna. Morphine made the pupils constrict, while atrophine made them dilate; so a careful balance of the two disguised the symptoms of poisoning. She discovered this method when it was used in the much-publicized case of Dr Robert Buchanan of New York City who murdered his wife for the insurance money in 1892. He went to the electric chair in Sing Sing in July 1895.

By then Toppan had been dismissed by Massachusetts General for recklessly dispensing opiates and was nursing two new victims, Israel and Lovey Dunham, her elderly landlords, back in Cambridge. Mr Dunham died in May 1895. The cause of death was give as a 'strangulated hernia'. Mrs Dunham died two years later of 'old age'. Then in 1899, Jane killed her foster sister Elizabeth who was married to the deacon of the Lowell Church, Oramel Brigham. She also killed the widower's housekeeper, Florence Calkins. Cause of death: 'chronic diabetes'.

Wealthy widow Mary McNear died after just three hours of nursing, apparent of 'apoplexy' and, a month later, old friend Myra Conners died so Jane could take her job as the dining hall matron at Lowell Theological School. She was then fired when financial irregularities were discovered.

Toppan's killing spree reached new heights in 1901. She poisoned new landlords Melvin and Eliza Beedle early that year, but only enough to make them ill. She then drugged their housekeeper, Mary Sullivan, to make her appear drunk so she could steal her job. Then she killed the entire Davis family in two months that summer.

Jane was living in a house rented from the family at Cataumet. When Mattie Davis turned up to collect the rent on a sweltering July day, Toppan gave her a glass of mineral water. She fell ill. Toppan nursed her over the next seven days, dosing her with morphine. By the time she died, her daughter Genevieve Gordon was ill and Mattie's widower, retired sea captain Alden Davis, begged her to stay on to nurse her. She died three weeks after her mother. Alden died two weeks later. The surviving daughter, Minnie Gibbs, refused to sign off the rental debt that Toppan owed the family. After drinking a tonic given to her by the nurse, Minnie died too.

Toppan then returned to Lowell, where she had designs on marrying Oramel Brigham. She killed his older sister, Edna Barrister, fearing she might get in the way. Oramel was also poisoned, so that Toppan might get close to him while nursing him back to health.

When Minnie's husband, Captain Paul Gibbs, returned from sea, he became suspicious that the entire, seemingly healthy Davis family had perished so suddenly. He spoke to the police, who called in toxicologist Leonard Wood and had the bodies exhumed.

Disappointed that her plan to marry Brigham had not worked out, Toppan overdosed on morphine and Brigham threw her out. She went to the home of George Nichols in Amherst, New Hampshire, to nurse his sister Sarah. There she was arrested for the murder of Minnie Gibbs. She voluntarily returned to Massachusetts, though protested her innocence.

When she was interviewed by a psychiatrist, she could not resist boasting about how many she had killed. On 23 June 1902, after an eight-hour trial, Toppan was declared not guilty by reason of insanity and sentenced to Taunton State Hospital for life. She died there at the age of eighty-four on 17 August 1938.

In a confession printed as a supplement to the *New York*

Journal, she claimed her murderous ways were sparked by being dumped when she was sixteen years old.

'If I had been a married woman, I probably would not have killed all of those people,' she said. 'I would have had my husband, my children and my home to take up my mind.'

Confession

Asked by her counsel 'how did you kill them?', Jane Toppan replied: 'I gave them doses of morphine and atrophine tablets in mineral water and sometimes in a dilution of whisky. Then I also used injections just as I did at Cataumet. I do not remember how I killed them all, but those that I recall were poisoned by atrophine and morphine. My memory is not good; I forget some things. No, I have absolutely no remorse. I have never felt sorry for what I have done. Even when I poisoned my dearest friends, as the Davises were, I did not feel any regret afterward. I do not feel any remorse now. I have thought it all over, and I cannot detect the slightest bit of sorrow over what I have done.'

BELLE GUNNESS

Hell's Belle *USA, 1900–08*

A fire at a farm in La Porte, Indiana, led to the discovery of one of the greatest serial killers in America. The fire uncovered evidence that as many as forty people had been killed on the farm. The perpetrator, Belle Gunness, was at first thought to have been one of the victims of the fire. Her former field hand and probable jealous lover Ray Lamphere was convicted of arson. But although the jury insisted the adult body found in the ashes was that of Gunness, he was acquitted of her murder.

Belle Sorenson – as she then was known – arrived in La Porte in 1901. A widow, she already seemed to be dogged by bad luck. The tale is told that at the age of eighteen in her native Norway, she had been kicked in the stomach while pregnant and had lost the child. The man responsible was from a rich family and avoided prosecution, but died soon after.

Arriving in the US four years later, Brynhild Paulsdatter Størseth anglicized her forename to Belle. In Chicago in 1884, she married Mads Sorenson. They opened a confectionery store together and had four children. Two died in infancy from colitis, the symptoms being similar to those of poisoning. Myrtle and Lucy survived their early years and the Sorensons adopted another girl named Jennie Olsen.

The Sorensons' confectionery business did not go well, but the building burnt down and they collected the insurance. Then Mads died. The cause of death on his death certificate was a heart attack, but there was some suspicion that he had been poisoned with strychnine. Further insurance policies brought Belle another $8,000 which she used to buy a farm in La Porte.

A woman with a fashionably curvaceous figure, Belle had no problem attracting men. As soon as she was settled, Peter Gunness arrived and married her. Then bad luck struck again. First Gunness's child from a previous marriage died – as did Gunness himself, hit improbably by a heavy meat grinder falling from a shelf. Again, there was insurance money to collect.

Belle had a high turnover of farmhands, who may also have been suitors. One of them had designs on Belle's adopted daughter Jennie, who then disappeared, ostensibly to go to college in California. Ray Lamphere was taken on and Belle lavished gifts on him. But she needed men with money. So she advertised in the personal ads of the big city papers. One ad said: 'Comely widow who owns a large farm in one of the finest districts in La Porte County, Indiana, desires to make the acquaintance of a gentleman equally well provided, with view of joining fortunes. No replies by letter considered unless sender is willing to follow answer with personal visit. Triflers need not apply.' Another read: 'WANTED: A woman who owns a beautifully located and valuable farm in first class condition, wants a good and reliable man as partner in the same. Some little cash is required for which will be furnished first-class security.'

One of the respondents was Andrew Helgelian, a Swede from South Dakota. Lamphere was asked to vacate his room for Helgelian prior to the wedding. After only a week, Helgelian disappeared. Lamphere had been heard in bars making threats about him and Belle.

Belle then sacked Lamphere and took on Joe Maxson as his replacement. Joe reported Lamphere's harassment of his employer and Belle had to have Lamphere arrested. Afraid for her life, she visited an attorney to make a will, telling him: 'That man is out to get me, and I fear one of these nights he will burn my house to the ground.'

That night her house did catch fire. After trying to raise the rest of the household, Maxson escaped, jumping from an upstairs window in his underwear. In the ashes, the bodies of Belle's two remaining children and the headless corpse of a woman were found. Lamphere was arrested and charged with arson and murder.

Having read about the fire, Andrew Helgelian's brother Asle turned up, bringing with him dozens of letters from Belle, begging Andrew to come to Indiana and bring money. Before leaving home, Andrew had withdrawn all his savings from the Bank of South Dakota.

In one letter she had written: 'Do not send any cash money through the bank. Banks cannot be trusted nowadays. Change all the cash you have into paper bills, largest denomination you can get, and sew them real good and fast on the inside of your underwear. Be careful and sew it real good, and be sure do not tell anyone of it, not even to your nearest relative. Let this only be a secret between us two and no one else. Probably we will have many other secrets, do you not think?'

Asle joined the team who were digging through the rubble and had already unearthed men's watches, wallets and other valuables. He asked Joe Maxson if Belle had dug any holes on the property to bury rubbish; Maxson replied that there was one which Belle had recently asked him to cover over.

Once they had cleared away the topsoil, the stench became unbearable. Next, the team unearthed pieces of a man's body. Asle recognized his brother's face. They continued digging and found more body parts belonging to two men and two women, including Jennie Olsen.

OTHER VICTIMS

The residents of La Porte soon realized that other people had gone missing. Ole Budsberg had last been seen in La Porte Savings Bank, mortgaging his land in Wisconsin. Recent immigrant Olaf Lindbloe had last been seen working on the

Gunness farm. Belle said he had left to go to St Louis to see the World's Fair. She also complained of being let down by farmhand Henry Gurholt who had gone off with a horse trader, she said. Others had come and gone so quickly that no one in town had got to know them.

Then there were the men she had culled from the small ads. One had left so quickly he had left behind his horse and buggy, one of a number on the farm. Joe Moe from Minnesota had brought $1,000 to pay off her mortgage. He disappeared in a week. Nevertheless, she asked George Anderson from Missouri to pay her mortgage too. That night, she appeared in his bedroom with such a sinister look on her face that he fled.

However, Gunness was not in custody, Lamphere was. The case against him depended entirely on whether the headless corpse found in the ashes was that of Belle Gunness. Testimony was given that the body was much smaller than Belle's. However, bridgework made up for Belle was identified by the local dentist, as it had been miraculously undamaged by the fire.

Evidence was also presented that the charred corpses had been found in the cellar, meaning they were already dead when the fire broke out, but strychnine from Andrew Helgelian's stomach had contaminated the other evidence. Then a witness said they had seen Belle with another women before the fire. Others said they had seen Belle with another man afterwards.

Convicted for arson, Lamphere was given two sentences of twenty years, but died after just one year in jail, still maintaining that Belle was 'out there somewhere'. Indeed, sightings continued into the 1930s.

After Andrew Helgelian disappeared, letters from Belle Gunness were found at his farm in Aberdeen, South Dakota. One read:

To the Dearest Friend in the World: No woman in the world is happier than I am. I know that you are now to come to me and be my own. I can tell from your letters that you are the man I want. It does not take one long to tell when to like a person, and you I like better than anyone in the world, I know. Think how we will enjoy each other's company. You, the sweetest man in the whole world. We will be all alone with each other. Can you conceive of anything nicer? I think of you constantly. When I hear your name mentioned, and this is when one of the dear children speaks of you, or I hear myself humming it with the words of an old love song, it is beautiful music to my ears. My heart beats in wild rapture for you, My Andrew, I love you. Come prepared to stay forever.

JEANNE WEBER

The Ogress *France, 1905–08*

At least eight infants – including two of her own – were thought to have died at the hands of what the French press dubbed *L'Ogresse de la Goutte d'Or*, named after the district of Montmartre where she began her murderous career. She was charged with murder, tried three times, and acquitted each time. The death toll continued to rise until she was declared insane.

Born in the Breton port of Paimpol in 1874, Jeanne Weber left home to go to Paris at the age of fourteen. At eighteen she married and had three children. Her husband was an alcoholic and she, too, turned to drink. Two of her children died in her care – one seven years old, the other a baby of three months. Relatives accused her of strangling them, but she was acquitted.

In 2 March 1905, Weber was baby-sitting her sister-in-law's daughter, eighteen-month-old Georgette, when the child suddenly died. A doctor who examined her noted marks around her neck, but otherwise could not find a cause of death. Nine days later, when Weber returned to baby-sitting duties at her sister-in-law's, Georgette's older sister, two-year-old Suzanne, died of unexplained convulsions.

Two weeks after that, Weber was baby-sitting for her brother, when his daughter, seven-year-old Germaine, suffered a sudden attack of choking. Again, marks were found on her throat. The child died the following day when Weber returned. The cause of death was given as diphtheria. Four days later Weber's own son

Marcel died, ostensibly of diphtheria. Once again signs of strangulation were overlooked.

While the youngsters of the family were dying off fast, two of Weber's sisters-in-law accepted an invitation to dinner. The two women then went out shopping, leaving Weber's ten-year-old nephew Maurice in her care. Returning unexpectedly, they found Maurice gasping for breath with a crazed Weber standing over him menacingly. This time the significance of the marks on his throat was all too apparent.

By then two other children – Marcel Poyatos and Lucie Aléandré – had also died in her care. Charges were brought. Defended by renowned attorney Henri Robert, Weber appeared as a grieving mother. Leading forensic scientist Dr Leon Thoinot swung the jury in her favour, saying: 'Science cannot tell you how these children came to die, but everything points to a natural death and that the accused is innocent.' Weber was acquitted.

On 7 April 1907, a peasant named Bavouzet summoned a doctor from the town of Villedieu to attend his nine-year-old son Auguste. The child was dead. There were marks on his throat, hidden by the boy's collar that was buttoned tightly to the neck. The cause of death was given as convulsions. However, it was then discovered that his carer, who called herself Madame Moulinet, was in fact the notorious Jeanne Weber. A second post-mortem ascribed the child's death to strangulation.

Weber was arrested. Henri Robert called in Dr Thoinot again. He examined the body once more. Even though it was in a state of extreme decomposition, he proclaimed that the boy's death had been caused by typhoid and again Weber walked free.

She was then seen working as an orderly in a children's hospital in Faucombault. George Bonjean, president of the Society for the Protection of Children, then gave her a job in a children's home in Orgeville to 'make up for the wrongs that justice has inflicted upon an innocent woman'. She worked there under the name Marie Lemoine, but a few days after she was hired, she was caught choking a child. She was fired, but Bonjean, fearing he would be a laughing stock, kept quiet about the incident.

On her return to Paris, Weber was arrested as a vagrant and blurted out: 'I am the woman who killed the children in the Goutte d'Or.' But when she was brought before the Prefect of Police, she denied it. He sent her to the mental asylum in Nanterre, where she was found to be sane and released.

She became the mistress of a man named Joy and lived with him in his lodgings near Toul. Then she turned to prostitution, sleeping with the railway workers in Bar-le-Duc. She moved to Commercy with one of them and took a room in an inn run by a family named Poirot, where Weber helped with the housekeeping.

One night, Weber told Madame Poirot that her common-law husband was a brute who would beat her when he came home drunk and asked if she would let her ten-year-old son Marcel sleep with her. That way she would not be beaten.

In the night, another guest named Madame Curlet heard loud noises. She went to find out what was happening and discovered Weber straddling the boy. There was a blood-soaked handkerchief around his neck. Mme Curlet screamed and the Poirots came running. Monsieur Poirot had to hit Weber in the face three times to get her to release her grip, but Marcel was already dead.

This time Henri Robert and Dr Thoinot could not save her. She was declared insane and locked up in a hospital in Mareville, while France exploded with indignation at the doctors who had allowed her to roam free. She was credited with eight murders but may have killed as many as twenty. In 1910, two years after her committal, she hanged herself.

Signor Lombroso

News of Jeanne Weber's crimes crossed the Channel and on 13 May 1908, *The Times* reported that a French journalist had asked well-known Italian criminologist Signor Lombroso for his opinion of the character of Jeanne Weber. 'After dwelling on the insufficiency of the material at his disposal for forming a judgment, as it seems to have consisted merely of a photograph, Signor Lombroso said that if the portrait were a good one there could be no doubt of the abnormal nature of the woman. The round, small skull, flat forehead, and virile expression of the face confirmed that impression. In his opinion she was a hysterical subject with epileptical and *crétin* characteristics, and probably came from a *crétin* family. He considers that her pervert instincts are mainly active under the influence of alcohol . . .'

Her father responded in an interview in the *Petit Parisien*, saying that Jeanne was a good child, who never caused her parents any trouble. It was she who brought up all her brothers and sisters, and was very gentle with them. Her father thought she must then be mad or suffering from some disease.

MARTHA RENDELL

Child Poisoner *Australia, 1907–08*

Donning his black cap Acting Chief Justice McMillan told Martha Rendell that the jury had found her guilty of the most horrible crimes of which he had ever heard. Throughout the trial he had been astonished by her demeanour. He called her an extraordinary woman. Even as he passed the sentence of death, she looked anxiously about the court, but displayed little emotion. She would be the last woman to be hanged in Western Australia.

Born in 1871, Martha Rendell left home at sixteen, took lovers and had three illegitimate children before beginning a passionate affair with Thomas Morris, a married man. When the scandal broke, Morris and his family fled to Perth in 1900. Rendell abandoned her children and followed him.

In 1906, Morris's wife left him. He took custody of their five youngest children and set up home with Rendell in a squalid cottage in East Perth. In the face of grinding poverty, Morris was often away working, leaving Rendell in charge of five resentful children. Things got worse the following year when the four youngest children were struck down by diphtheria during a city-wide epidemic.

The family physician, Dr James Cuthbert, who later gave damning evidence against Rendell at the trial, commended her for her devotion to nursing the children, even at the expense of her own health. Nevertheless, that July, nine-year-old Annie died of 'epilepsy and cardiac weakness'. The other three were diagnosed with typhoid in August. Five-year-old Olive died in

October of 'haemorrhage and typhoid'. Less than two years later, in June 1908, fourteen-year-old Arthur began to exhibit the same symptoms as Olive – vomiting, diarrhoea and the swelling of the throat associated with diphtheria. When he died in October, doctors conducted an autopsy, which was halted by Rendell. Nevertheless, they noted ulceration of the bowels, haemorrhage and cardiac failure as the cause of death.

Fifteen-year-old George then sought refuge with his mother and elder brother. Thomas Morris reported him missing to the police. When they found him, George told the police that Rendell had murdered Arthur by painting his throat with spirit of salt – that is, hydrochloric acid. Arthur had told him so. However, at the time a dilute solution of hydrochloric acid was used as a mild antiseptic, sometimes applied to the throat in cases of diphtheria. When Rendell served George bitter cups of tea, he fled, fearing for his life.

The police got permission to exhume the bodies of the three dead children. Post-mortems found inflammation and haemorrhaging of the bowel, indicating that poison had been administered. However, no murder trial had involved the administration of hydrochloric acid before, so it was tried out on rabbits and guinea pigs to establish whether a trial could take place.

A coroner's court in August 1909 found there was sufficient evidence to charge Rendell with the wilful murder of Arthur Morris – and Thomas Morris was named as an accomplice as he had bought the spirit of salt.

At their trial in September 1909, little evidence was presented against them. But a neighbour said that, through a window, she had seen Rendell swabbing Arthur's throat while the child screamed and cried for help. When she visited the Morris home, she smelt the bottle, which gave off powerful fumes that provoked a burning sensation. But Rendell claimed the doctor had prescribed the medication.

The defence had no witnesses to call, though both Rendell and

Morris took the stand. In his summing up, Mr Justice McMillan reminded the jury they must put out of their minds any newspaper stories calculated to prejudice their minds and forget anything they had heard outside the court. He went on: 'It could not be disputed that at the time when the offence was alleged to have been committed, they were living a life of immorality. The husband Morris had turned his wife out and was living with the female accused, with whom he was reported to have been on intimate terms in one of the other states.'

Morris was acquitted, saved by the fact he was often away from home and would not have known what was going on. Rendell was convicted of wilful murder and given a mandatory death sentence. Petitions were presented to the government and speeches were made on her behalf in parliament. It did no good. Just twenty days after the sentence of death was made, Martha Rendell was hanged in Fremantle Prison, protesting her innocence.

Plea for clemency

On 26 September 1909, with a week to go before Martha Rendell's execution, Thomas Morris, the father of the murdered children, wrote to the *West Australian* with a passionate plea on her behalf.

To the Editor.

Sir, I pray you will grant me a small space in your valuable paper for this my appeal on behalf of Martha Rendell. I am away in the back blocks seeking work, having spent my last penny. All I possess, even my tools, were sold for my defence, so that I am powerless to do anything further than write to you on her behalf. I have waited until now, hoping someone would take the matter up. I do not know who is the proper person in authority to write to, so I appeal through the 'West Australian' to that person. I know that some of the evidence given against me was incorrect. Then why not the same against her? I also know now that evidence could have been called in support of our case but was not. I left everything to the lawyers, and no doubt they did their best with the money they had. But I say fearlessly, before God, I was innocent, and so is Martha Rendell. She was everything that was good and kind and attentive to my children and did everything for their benefit. I know her better than anyone else, and I say she was incapable of doing what is attributed to her. She may have appeared hard outwardly, but no woman ever had a more tender heart than she, and I say it would be a shame and disgrace to this country and humanity if the dread sentence were carried out, because I believe that sooner or later her innocence will be proved, and I feel I cannot keep silent and allow this injustice (for injustice it is, God knows) to be done to an innocent woman.

Yours, etc., THOMAS N. MORRIS.

ENRIQUETA MARTÍ

The Vampire of Barcelona *Spain, 1895–1912*

At the end of the nineteenth century, industrialization brought a flood of peasants into Barcelona while the business class grew wealthy on the backs of the poor. The rich could pay handsomely for anything they wanted, including sex. As a prostitute, Enriqueta Martí was happy to take their money. She also kidnapped children to provide them for paedophiles. Then she killed them to make costly beauty products and love potions.

At the age of twenty, Enriqueta Martí arrived at a railway station in Barcelona in 1888. She had answered an advertisement for a domestic servant placed by a wealthy family who lived in the upmarket Eixample area of the city. A lowly drudge, she quickly came to envy the lavish lifestyle of her employers.

Barcelona was holding a World's Fair that year and the luxury displayed there was in stark contrast to the grinding poverty of the slum districts such as El Raval, then known as El Chino. An attractive young woman, Enriqueta sought to better herself materially by quitting her domestic job and going to work as a prostitute in a high-class brothel. Among her numerous client were men of wealth and position.

In 1895, Enriqueta married the artist Juan Pujaló. It was not a happy marriage as Enriqueta could not resist the lure of her clients' money. The couple frequently broke up, splitting for good in 1907.

The economy of the port suffered a downturn with the Spanish-American War of 1898 during which the country lost its remaining colonies in the Americas and the Pacific. In the early 1900s, Martí rented a small apartment in El Chino, where she ran a brothel. Knowing the tastes of some wealthy men, she started kidnapping children and forcing them into prostitution. During the day, she would dress in rags and join bread queues, looking for abandoned waifs who she would clean up for her clients. It was a lucrative trade and, at night, she would don expensive clothing and jewellery to mingle with high society in the Casino de la Arrabassada and the Eliceu opera house. This brought her into contact with wealthy women. To expand her business, she began selling them herbal remedies and beauty products, which were made up in another of the chain of apartments she rented.

In 1909, the conscription of reservists to fight in the unpopular war in Morocco provoked a general strike and rioting. The government in Madrid sent in troops. Over a hundred civilians were killed in what became known as *La setmana tràgica* – 'Tragic Week'. Martial law was declared. Thousands were arrested and Martí's brothel was raided. She was arrested, along with a young client who was thought to have come from a wealthy family. Consequently, the case never came to trial.

Martí must have believed she was now above the law. At the time people believed that drinking blood was a cure of the tuberculosis that was rife in the city. Upper-class women also thought that children's blood preserved the bloom of youth and their fat would prevent ageing of the skin. Martí provided these. She also pounded bones into powder to make her expensive preparations.

Rumours began to circulate that young children were going missing. The authorities did nothing. The civil governor of Barcelona, Manuel Portela Valladares, even issued a statement in 1911 denying it was happening. The last thing he wanted was the intervention of the government in Madrid again.

On 10 February 1912, a young girl named Teresita Guitart Congost went missing. This time there was an outcry. Claudia Elías, a neighbour of Martí's, saw a girl answering Teresita's description peering out of her window. Martí, she knew, had no children, so Claudia went to the police.

When the police raided the flat on 27 February, they found two girls. Martí claimed that she had found Teresita the previous day, wandering the streets, lost and hungry. But Elías had seen the girl five days earlier. The other child, Angelita, Martí claimed was her own.

When the two girls were questioned, Teresita said that she had been lured by the promise of sweets. She was returned to her distraught parents. The questioning of the girls brought some very disturbing evidence to light. The girls said they had often been left on their own in the apartment. There was a room there that they were forbidden to enter. However, they did. In it they found a bag containing bloodstained clothes and a bloody knife. Angelita added that, before Teresita arrived, there had been a five-year-old boy called Pepito living there. One day, she had seen 'mama' stab him to death.

'Mama did not realize that I saw her take Pepito, put him on the dining table and kill him,' she said.

When he heard of Martí's arrest, Juan Pujaló went to the police, telling them that he and his wife had no children. It was later discovered that Martí had stolen Angelita at birth from his sister Maria – assisting at the delivery, Martí had convinced her that her baby was still-born.

The apartment was searched and the bag containing the clothing and knife were found, along with another bag containing the bones of children. In another locked room, the police found pitchers and a washbasin containing the raw materials – blood, fat and bones – along with jars containing the finished products, labelled for sale.

Three other flats rented by Martí were raided and more jars were found. False walls and ceilings also hid human remains. More remains of children as young as three were found buried in the garden at one of the properties. The police also seized a book of recipes compiled by Martí, along with a list of her wealthy clients.

Martí admitted procuring for paedophiles, but it was her clients that were monsters, not her. The women who bought her tonics and creams knew what they were made from, but were unconcerned as they considered street children as trash. She was simply a businesswoman, supplying a demand.

There was intense interest in the names on Martí's list of clientele. However, the date of her trial kept being put back. Eventually it was announced that she had died in the Reina Amàlia jail on 12 May 1913, after a long illness – though some believe that she had been hanged in the prison yard by her fellow prisoners who had been paid by her wealthy clients to do so.

Testimony

After Martí was arrested, the national newspapers carried daily stories about the case under the headline 'The Mysteries of Barcelona'. Some testimony came from a peasant woman from Alcañiz who had just arrived in Barcelona with a baby in her arms to find work. The woman felt faint from hunger and sat on the doorstep of a house. A stranger approached her.

'What a pretty babe, do you want me to give her a little breast?' she asked.

The women declined, saying the child no longer suckled. The stranger then offered to buy the woman a glass of milk. On the way to the dairy, the stranger offered to carry the child.

When the woman was drinking the milk, the stranger said it would be better with bread and left to get some, taking the baby. She never came back. Six years later, the woman from Alcañiz identified the woman who had taken her baby as Enriqueta Martí, the Vampire of Barcelona.

AMY ARCHER-GILLIGAN

Arsenic and Old Lace *USA, 1907–17*

The activities of serial killers are hardly material for comedy – particularly those of Amy Archer-Gilligan who is estimated to have killed at least twenty people and perhaps as many as a hundred. Yet, twenty years after the case was closed, New York playwright Joseph Kesselring used the story as the basis for the play *Arsenic and Old Lace*, which ran for three-and-a-half years on Broadway. Frank Capra then made it into a classic movie, starring Cary Grant.

Amy Duggan was born in Milton, Connecticut, in 1873. In 1897, she married James Archer and the couple had a baby daughter. Four years later, they moved to Newington, Connecticut, to work as live-in carers for elderly widower John Seymour. He died in 1904. The Archers stayed on in the house as tenants, making money by running the boarding house as Sister Amy's Nursing Home for the Elderly.

After three years, the Seymour family decided to sell the house and the Archers moved on to Windsor, where they bought a brick house at 37 Prospect Street. There they started the Archer Home for Elderly and Infirm. They ran the home together until 1910, when Mr Archer died of Bright's disease, a catch-all phrase for kidney failure of unknown cause.

In 1913, Mrs Archer married again, this time to Michael Gilligan. The marriage lasted just three months until Gilligan died of 'acute bilious attack' – that is, very bad indigestion – leaving her an estate of $4,000. It began to be noticed that many of the residents of the Archer Home for the Elderly and Infirm did not last long – particularly those who paid a flat fee of $1,000 (worth over $24,000 in 2017) for care as long as they lived. Others paid weekly and survived.

Deaths at the Archer home passed without investigation. After all, its inmates were elderly. Then Nellie Pierce, sister of sixty-one-year-old Franklin R. Andrews, grew suspicious about his death. On the morning of 29 May 1914, he had been seen working on the lawn at the Archer house. He was dead before midnight.

When she went through her dead brother's papers, she discovered that Mrs Archer-Gilligan was badgering him for money. She went to the district attorney, to no avail. So she approached the *Hartford Courant* who began their own investigation.

The newspaper discovered that, since the care home had opened in 1907, there had been sixty deaths – forty-eight of them since 1911. This was a shockingly high mortality rate as only ten or twelve people lived at the home at any one time.

The authorities then began to take an interest. On 2 May 1916, Andrews' body was exhumed and traces of arsenic were found. This led to other bodies – including that of Mr Gilligan – being dug up too.

A week later, the state police went to the Archer home to ask Mrs Archer-Gilligan about the high death rate. She replied: 'Well, we didn't ask them to come here but we do the best we can for them. They are old people, and some live for a long time while others die after being here a short time.'

Questioned about the financial arrangements she made with the residents, she said she barely scraped by: 'I am a poor, hard-working woman and I can't understand why I am persecuted as I have been during the last few years. This is a Christian work and one that is very trying as we have to put up with lots of things on account of the peculiarities of the old people.'

When she was arrested, she protested, saying: 'I will prove my innocence, if it takes my last mill. I am not guilty and I will hang before they prove it.'

The following day, the front page of the *Hartford Courant* carried the headline: 'Police believe Archer home for aged a murder factory.'

The story said: 'The arrest of the Windsor woman yesterday is the result of the suspicions aroused when Mrs Nellie E. Pierce of No. 205 Vine St., Hartford, found in the effects of her brother, Franklin R. Andrews, after he died at the Archer house, a letter from Mrs Archer-Gilligan asking for a loan, "as near $1,000 as possible," about which the woman had said nothing to her.'

When Pierce asked Archer-Gilligan about the loan, she denied receiving one, at first. Later, she said she had received $500 as a gift. After Pierce had hired a lawyer to demand the return of the money, Archer-Gilligan paid it back, 'not because she could not keep it but because she did not feel it worth quarreling over,' the *Courant* reported.

Reporters also discovered that Archer-Gilligan had also purchased large amounts of morphine and arsenic. Another of the bodies to be exhumed was that of Alice Graham Gowdy, who had died at the age of sixty-nine. She and her seventy-one-year-old husband Loren B. Gowdy had enquired about moving into the Archer home in May 1914. They wanted to move into the room formerly occupied by Andrews on 1 June. Andrews' death certificate was signed on 30 May. The Gowdys got a telegram the following day, saying they could move in after paying a fee of $1,000. Mrs Gowdy died on 4 December. When exhumed, her body showed traces of arsenic. After his wife's death, Mr Gowdy lived long enough to testify at Archer-Gilligan's trial two years later.

While the authorities thought she had killed at least twenty, Archer-Gilligan was indicted for the poisoning murders of five people: Andrews; Alice Gowdy; her second husband, Michael Gilligan; Charles A. Smith, who died on 9 April 1914; and Maud Howard Lynch, who died on 2 February 1916. All but Lynch died of arsenic poisoning. She was poisoned by strychnine. However, Archer-Gilligan was tried only for the murder of Andrews.

The trial began on 21 June 1917, in Hartford. It drew large crowds and was covered widely in the press. She was found guilty and sentenced to death by hanging. However, on appeal, it was found that the trial judge had made an error and a retrial was ordered.

This time her defence was insanity. A forensic psychiatrist said she was crazy and her nineteen-year-old daughter, Mary E. Archer, testified that she was a morphine addict. The trial ended abruptly when she changed her plea to guilty of second-degree murder, which brought a life sentence.

Archer-Gilligan began her sentence at the state prison in Wethersfield. Five years later, she was declared insane and transferred to the Connecticut Valley Hospital at Middletown. There she was described as a quiet and cooperative patient. When she died in 1962 at the age of ninety-four, the *Courant* reported: 'Mostly she sat in a chair, dressed in a black dress trimmed with lace, a Bible on her lap, and prayed.'

In the play and film *Arsenic and Old Lace*, the 'Connecticut Borgia' was transformed into two sisters. The victims were aged men who lived in their boarding house and the old-fashioned murder weapon of choice was elderberry wine, spiked with arsenic.

Not guilty?

The Windsor Historical Society maintains a file on Amy Archer-Gilligan. When Ruth Bonito from the historical society of nearby Windsor Locks checked it out, she concluded that Amy may have been innocent. She never confessed to the crimes and the evidence against her was circumstantial. She did buy arsenic, but said it was to kill rats. True, the home she ran did have a high mortality rate, but that did not prove that the inmates were poisoned.

It was also true that arsenic was found in the bodies that had been exhumed. However, arsenic was once used extensively by American embalmers, a fact confirmed by Connecticut's state archaeologist Nicholas Bellantoni. Mrs Bonito also pointed out that Mrs Archer-Gilligan was a church-going woman who donated a stained-glass window to a Windsor church – hardly the type of woman to turn to serial killing in middle age.

TILLIE KLIMEK

Mrs Bluebeard *USA, 1912–22*

Reputed to be a psychic, Tillie Klimek claimed to have precognitive dreams, during which she could foresee when her husbands were going to die. All three of her husbands died within the space of just one year – something she put down to her bad luck with men and her ominous dreams. When she was eventually arrested for the attempted murder of Joseph Klimek on 26 October 1922 – over eight years after her first husband's death – she told the arresting officer: 'The next one I want to cook a dinner for is you.' Convicted of killing her third husband by putting arsenic in his food and moonshine and the attempted murder of her fourth, she was also suspected of having done away with her first two husbands and a boyfriend. The press dubbed her 'The Polish Borgia' and 'Mrs Bluebeard'. But her four husbands were just the start of her career in poisoning.

B orn Ottilie Gburek in Poland in 1876, she came to the United States at the age of one. The family settled in the north side of Chicago in an area known as Little Poland – at the time, the city with the second largest Polish population in the world, after Warsaw.

She married her first husband Joseph Mitkiewicz when she was just fourteen in 1890. In January 1914, she predicted his death, reportedly giving the exact date of his demise a few weeks hence. He fell ill and died just as she had foreseen. The death certificate gave the cause of death as a heart attack. She collected a life insurance cheque for $1,000.

Marrying again almost immediately, Tillie's second husband, John Ruskowski, lasted just three months, again dying on the date she predicted. He left $1,900 in cash and life insurance. A boyfriend, Joseph Guszkowski, was the next to die after jilting her. It seems that she admitted poisoning her first two husbands, which persuaded him to leave, but she threatened to accuse him under the Mann Act that made the interstate trafficking of women for immoral purposes a felony. Then he died, as she had predicted.

With Guszkowski out of the way, her third (or fourth) husband, Frank Kupszcyk, moved in. He lasted two years until Tillie had another of her premonitions. She told neighbours that he 'would not live long' and he only had 'two inches to live' and she even taunted Frank himself, telling him, 'You'll be dying soon' and 'It won't be long now.' He died on 25 April 1921. Sitting beside his deathbed, she sewed the hat she would wear at the funeral and had taken the precaution of buying a cheap coffin for $30, which she stored in the basement.

When he did eventually die, she did not bother to act the grieving widow – she played upbeat dance music on a phonograph in the same room as the corpse to celebrate. His death netted her $675 from life insurance and at the funeral she reached into the open coffin, tugged his ear and said: 'You devil, you won't get up anymore.'

Not one to hang around, she married Joseph Klimek later that year despite the admonitions of his friends and family. By then, neighbours were getting rather wary of her premonitions and began to shun her. However, she told her cousin Nellie Sturmer Koulik, who had also lost a husband, that the marriage was not working out. When Nellie suggested a divorce, Tillie replied that she would 'get rid of him some other way'. It was, allegedly, Nellie who supplied the poison 'Rough on Rats' – in which arsenic was the active ingredient.

Following Tillie's prediction of his demise, Joseph fell ill. His brother John suspected foul play, especially as two of Joseph's dogs had just died. He related his suspicions to the doctor who diagnosed the symptoms of arsenic poisoning. Joseph was rushed to hospital where, after three months' recuperation, he pulled through.

DEATHS IN THE FAMILY

Tillie Klimek's cousin, Rose Chudzinski, was suspicious about other deaths in the family. Three cousins had all died in the space of a few years: sixteen-year-old Stanley Zakrzewski had died in 1912, twenty-three-year-old Stelle Zakrzewski in 1913 and fifteen-year-old Helen Zakrzewski in 1915. Tillie had nursed them all in their final illness and again had premonitions of their deaths from a deadly plague.

Nellie's infant daughter Sophie Sturmer died in 1917. Her twin brother Ben died a month later. Then in 1918, Nellie's first husband passed away, followed by her two-year-old grand-daughter Dorothy Spera, who had been in her grandmother Nellie's care at the time. A man named Meyers, thought to be another sweetheart of Tillie's, went mysteriously missing. And two neighbours – Stelle Grantowiske and Rose Split – reportedly died after eating candy she had given them, following an argument.

Some survived. Nellie's son John Sturmer fell ill after his father's death. He recovered but was convinced his mother had tried to poison him. His sister, Lillian Sturmer, lived with Klimek for about a year when she was thirteen. She fell ill and, although she survived, she suffered from heart trouble for the rest of her life.

Cousin Nick Micko and Frank Klimek's sister-in-law Bessie Kupszcyk also sampled Tillie's cooking and fell ill. A neighbour's dog that Tillie found a nuisance was not so lucky. It died. In total seven family members mysteriously died and four survived their unexpected illnesses.

The police then received an anonymous letter and Frank Kupszcyk's body was exhumed and found to be full of arsenic, as was that of Wojek Sturmer. The letter also named Nellie Koulik, who was arrested one week after her cousin. She had been having an affair with Albert Koulik, who became her second husband after her first husband and the children had died. Both Tillie and Nellie were charged with murder.

Soon other family members were implicated. Nellie's sister Cornelia was also arrested when her son-in-law accused her of poisoning him. Other local women were also arrested in what Assistant State Attorney W. F. McLaughlin called 'the most astonishing wholesale poisoning plot ever uncovered'. However, they had to be released when no evidence for a conspiracy could be found.

In custody Tillie was cold and showed no emotion, while taunting Nellie that she was going to be hanged. Tillie protested her innocence.

When the trial started on 27 February 1923, Joseph Klimek told the court that his food had tasted funny and that his wife had badgered him into taking out more life insurance. Tillie Klimek insisted that she had not murdered her husbands and that Frank had died of alcoholic poisoning. And yet arsenic was found in all their bodies.

While Tillie was found to wilful and conniving, Nellie was thought to be simple-minded. Even though her children gave evidence against her, Nellie was acquitted. The jury even found her not guilty of supplying Klimek the rat poison she had used to kill so many.

Tillie Klimek was found guilty of murdering Frank Kupszcyk, but was spared the gallows because no woman had ever been hanged in Illinois. She was sentenced to life imprisonment without parole, the harshest sentence ever given to a woman in Cook County. She died in prison in November 1936.

The sentence

To receive the sentence of life imprisonment from Judge Marcus Kavanagh, Tillie Klimek was wearing a new black dress and the same black silk hat she wore on the day she followed the coffin containing the body of her third husband to the cemetery.

This is one of the most remarkable cases in the history of criminology [Judge Kavanagh said]. The books do not contain another case like it. We have here a woman of average intelligence, a modern housewife and a good cook. When she is among women she is affectionate and, it is said, she is the most popular woman in the jail. Yet, the testimony showed, cold-bloodedly, without feeling or remorse, she killed three of her husbands and attempted to kill a fourth.

If this woman was let loose today, she would kill another man. She has a desire to see men with whom she was intimate suffer. Criminologists tell us there are a few such people on this earth. I venture to say there are more husbands poisoned in this community than the police or authorities realize. But the knowledge that Tillie Klimek has gone down will stay their hands.

SUSAN NEWELL

Last Woman to Be Hanged in Scotland
Scotland, 1923

A lorry driver saw a woman and child struggling with a ladened handcart in Coatbridge, Lanarkshire, in June 1923 and gave them a lift. He dropped them off in Duke Street, Glasgow. As they got down, a woman in a nearby house saw a little foot, then a head, pop out of the bundle on the cart. These were quickly covered up. But it was too late. A chase ensued and the woman was apprehended. Asked by the police to explain what she was doing with the body of a small boy on her cart, the woman said: 'It was not me who did it. It was my husband.'

Three weeks earlier, twenty-nine-year-old Susan Newell and her husband John had moved into rooms in Newlands Street, Coatbridge. Soon, their landlady Annie Young was left with no choice but to ask them to leave because of their non-stop arguing. Mrs Newell also made a complaint to the police about her husband assaulting her and told her landlady that he beat her daughter Janet. Her husband was a drunkard and a womanizer.

On the evening of Wednesday, 20 June 1923, Janet was playing out in the street when paperboy John Johnson turned up at the Newells' one-room apartment. Mrs Young and friends in the kitchen below then heard three thumps, which they took to be the sound of Mrs Newell packing. A few minutes later, Mrs Newell popped down to the kitchen to ask Mrs Young if she had a box. She hadn't.

At eleven that night, John's father reported his thirteen-year-old son missing. His body was recovered the next day from the bundle Mrs Newell had been pushing on the handcart. A post-mortem gave the cause of death as strangulation – with such force that his spine had been dislocated. Marks were also found suggesting the impact of a blunt instrument on the head – more than one blow – and burning. It was later discovered that his head had been thumped against a lit gas ring.

Mrs Newell claimed that she had had a row with her husband the previous night. He had been about to strike her when the paperboy screamed, and so her husband grabbed him and choked him until he was black in the face. She fainted. When she came to, the boy was dead and her husband was gone. She rolled the body up in a mat and made for Glasgow the following morning.

Six-year-old Janet told the police that she had seen the boy go into the house. Asked what had happened to him, she said: 'My daddy choked him with his hands and he died.'

John Newell was in Haddington near Edinburgh when he read of his wife's arrest in the *Scotsman*. He went straight to the police station and was arrested. When cautioned, he said he knew nothing about the murder and that he had not been in Coatbridge from Tuesday until Wednesday night. He claimed the reason for his absence was that, after he had attended his brother's funeral, his wife had assaulted him in the street, head-butting him twice in the face. He had even gone to the police station in Coatbridge at 10.30 p.m. on Wednesday as there was a warrant out for his arrest for deserting his wife, though he was not arrested.

Even though he had been back in Coatbridge that evening he had not returned home. Instead, after visiting family members, he had stayed in a lodging house before heading to Haddington. Nevertheless, he was charged with murder and sent for trial alongside his wife. Both pleaded not guilty – John on the strength of his alibi, Susan claiming insanity on the day of the crime.

In the witness box, Janet changed her story. Her stepfather

had not been at home at the time of the murder, she said, and it was her mother who had told her to say that he had choked the little boy. This cleared John Newell. Other witnesses supported his alibi and the prosecution withdrew the charges.

Expert witnesses called by the prosecution said that they could see no signs of insanity in Susan Newell. The defence argued that she was under great stress at the time – deserted by her husband without a penny and about to be turned out on the streets – reducing the offence to culpable homicide. The jury rejected this and found her guilty of murder. The judge sentenced her to death. She showed no emotion as she stepped down from the dock. However, when she was told that her plea for a reprieve had been rejected by the Home Office, she fainted.

In Duke Street Prison, not far from where she had been arrested, she refused the white cap normally put over the head of the condemned. Death was instantaneous and the hangman said she was 'very brave'. Outside a crowd of two hundred, mostly women, held a vigil. Janet was sent to be brought up in a convent.

The daughter's testimony

Susan Newell's daughter, six-year-old Janet MacLeod, was called for the prosecution by advocate Lord Kinross. She had previously told the police: 'My daddy choked him with his hands and he died.' The child was naturally overawed by the packed courtroom and the distinguished legal men in their wigs and gowns. But once she calmed down, she had a different tale to tell.

She said she recalled the boy going up the stairs to her house while she was playing outside. She did not see him come down again. Later her mammy took her to Duffy's public house. She had a jug with her and went into the pub, leaving Janet outside. Her mother then came out with beer in the jug and was also carrying whisky and wine. The damning testimony then elicited a series of questions:

KINROSS: 'Where did you go when you got home?'

JANET: 'Into the room.'

KINROSS: 'Did you see anything?'

JANET: 'A little wee boy dead on the couch.'

KINROSS: 'How did you know he was dead?'

JANET: 'I went over to look.'

KINROSS: 'What did your mother say?'

JANET: '"Keep quiet."'

KINROSS: 'Did your mother do anything?'

JANET: 'She drank the beer.'

KINROSS: 'What did she do?'

JANET: 'She took my father's drawers and put them over his face. His nose was bleeding. She got a poker to get the floor up to try to get the wee boy in, and we tried to get a box from Mrs Young.'

KINROSS: 'The same night, where did you sleep?'

JANET: 'In the house.'

Janet said she did not see her stepfather that day. The day before he had gone to a funeral and he had not come back.

KINROSS: 'There were two ladies who spoke to you on this happening. Did you tell them the same as you told us today?'

JANET: 'No. I forget what I told them.'

KINROSS: 'Do you remember telling them it was your daddy who choked the boy?'

JANET: 'Yes.'

KINROSS: 'Why did you tell them that?'

JANET: 'Mammy told me.'

KINROSS: 'That is what she told you to say?'

JANET: 'Yes.'

VERA RENCZI

Man Slaughterer *Romania, 1920–25*

The story of Vera Renczi was reported by the European correspondents of American newspapers in 1925. It was compelling. A seductive beauty, she had killed two husbands, thirty-two lovers and her own ten-year-old son and kept their bodies in zinc coffins in the cellar of her home.

V era was a wayward young lady. As a teenager, she often ran off with her latest flame, only to return when she had tired of him. Her father must have been relieved when she fell for a wealthy businessman, many years her senior, named Karl Schick. After a honeymoon in the Tyrol, they settled in a large mansion outside the city of Berkerekul in Serbia and, fourteen months later, they had a son whom they named Lorenzo.

Vera began to suspect that her husband was being unfaithful and poisoned him by putting arsenic in his dinner. She told people that he had gone away on business, later confiding to friends that he had left her and run off without even leaving a note. Meanwhile, she lavished all her attention on her son.

After a year, tongues began to wag. Vera had been seen out in the company of various young men. One of them was a ne'er-do-well named Josef Renczi, to whom she became as devoted as she had been to her first husband. She then announced that she had just heard that her husband had been killed in a car accident, allowing her to marry Renczi. Although she settled down to become a dutiful wife, Renczi continued to have a roving eye. Four months later, he too disappeared, ostensibly on a long trip and, after a year, she said she had received a note saying that he was not coming back.

Vera did not marry again, but that did not diminish her interest in men. In the evenings, she would visit the cafés and nightspots of Berkerekul, where she was known as the 'Mysterious Huntress'. She would seek out young men who were strangers in town and take them home. They would not be seen again. After she had had what she wanted from them, it was thought that she sent them back to their own country.

REBELLIOUS NATURE

Sources say that Vera was born in Bucharest, Romania, in 1903, though as it was reported that she was thirty when she faced trial for multiple murder in 1925, it is likely to have been earlier than that. She moved with her father to Berkerekul – now Zrenjanin – in Serbia around 1916. The tale is told that, after her father had given her a dog, it was found dead in the garden. Asked how it had died, Vera said she had poisoned it. Asked why, she said that she had overheard her father offering to give the dog to one of their neighbours because it barked too much at night and she was not going to let anyone else have it. Her father reproved her for her jealousy and gave her a thrashing.

This did not curb her rebellious nature. Already a beauty from a young age, she was seldom seen unaccompanied by a boyfriend and when she had just turned fifteen she was found in the dormitory of a nearby boys' school at midnight.

Things went wrong when Vera seduced a young banker named Leo Pachich who had recently married. He tried to break off their affair as his wife was pregnant, but he was persuaded to stay for one last meal. It was, indeed, his last.

When he did not return from what she had been told was a short business trip, his wife made enquiries at his office to be told that there was no business trip. She went to the police, but as there was no suspicion of foul play there was nothing they could do.

Mrs Pachich began making enquiries of her own and discovered that he had been seen in a café in Berkerekul in the company of a beautiful blonde. When she told the police, they had no doubt who the blonde was. At the wife's insistence, they went to question Vera.

She was frank. The missing banker had been her lover. But as he was married to someone she detested, she had told him to get dressed and go. She had not seen him since. The story, though sordid, was thoroughly plausible.

Mrs Pachich was not content with this. She made further enquiries and came up with a list of other men who had been seen in Vera's company, then disappeared, and she urged the police to search her house. Fearing that the reputation of their city was at stake, the police acted quickly. They surrounded the Renczi château and broke into the cellar. To get there they had to go down long vaulted stone corridors and break through three iron doors. An old woman servant resisted their entry fiercely and they were obliged to handcuff her. At last they reached a huge, vaulted cellar and found thirty-five zinc coffins, each of them bearing the name of the occupant, arranged around the walls. All of the occupants were males. In the middle of the room stood an easy chair.

Madame Renczi was arrested in her luxurious boudoir. Taken before an examining magistrate, at first she denied everything, claiming that the bodies in the cellar were those of friends and townspeople who had been killed by the Germans during the First World War. Further investigation of the background of the victims proved this was not true and in a secret compartment behind the wall of her boudoir they found enough arsenic to kill a hundred men. Arsenic was common in Serbia at the time; it was a by-product of mines producing metal ores in the area. In the face of such evidence, she confessed.

The *American Weekly* of 22 August 1925 carried what purports to be her confession. It read:

My first husband was the one who made me madly jealous of other women. I couldn't endure the idea of his ever looking at them! And after a year I felt that he would soon turn away from me, not entirely, but just enough to make me jealous. I swore to myself that he would never belong to another woman. So I killed him.

My second husband did not last as long. I was obliged to kill him after four months because he talked to other women. From that time on it became a disease with me. I wanted young men. Yet once I possessed them I could not bear the idea that any other woman might come after me.

I had the power to tantalize them. They would follow me. Then, perhaps a week after they had remained with me at my house, I would notice that they grew either distracted or would say something about having to return home. I would consider these first signs the beginning of the end. And, consequently, my first burst of passion for them would be followed by jealousy, and I would poison them without waiting any further.

Asked why she had killed all these human beings, she said: 'They were men. I could not endure the thought that they would ever put their arms around another woman after they had embraced me.'

'But you also murdered your own son,' said the magistrate.

Apparently, he had stumbled on the coffins in the cellar.

'He had threatened to betray me,' she said. 'He was a man, too. Soon he would have held another woman in his arms.'

'And the easy chair?'

'I liked to go down there in the evening and sit among my victims, gloating over their fate.'

She was sentenced to death, but this was automatically commuted to life imprisonment. Vera Renczi died in a mental institution in 1939.

BONNIE PARKER

Bonnie & Clyde *USA, 1933–34*

No one knows how many people Bonnie Parker killed. Sometime member of the Barrow gang, W.D. Jones, said that he never saw her shoot at a law officer. But he quit the gang in September 1933. Two months later she was indicted for murder by a grand jury and a warrant issued for her arrest. Her photograph had already appeared on a 'Wanted for Murder' poster in April, then again in June. After the killing of two highway patrolmen in April 1934, a reward was put on her head. Another arrest warrant for murder with her name on it was issued after the slaying of another officer. In an era known for its violent criminals, she was up there with 'Machine Gun' Kelly, 'Baby Face' Nelson, 'Pretty Boy' Floyd, John Dillinger and Ma Baker.

After the Wall Street stock market crash of 1929, the US suffered the Great Depression. It was a lawless time with gangsters such as Al Capone, made rich by bootlegging during Prohibition, ruling the roost in the cities. Meanwhile bank robbers and stick-up men such as John Dillinger, Baby Face Nelson and Pretty Boy Floyd took to the road. But the most romantic of these villains was the couple Bonnie Parker and Clyde Barrow who were seen, albeit briefly, as the Robin Hoods of their day.

Born in 1910, Bonnie was just four when her father died. She did well at school, but at the age of sixteen she married Roy Thornton. They lived together sporadically as he was often on the run from the law and they separated permanently when he was sentenced to five years in jail for robbery in 1929.

Working as a waitress in Dallas, Bonnie longed for excitement. It arrived in the form of twenty-one-year-old Clyde Barrow, who had been a criminal since the age of seventeen. They lived together briefly before he was sentenced to two years for robbery. In March 1930, he escaped from Waco jail with the aid of a pistol, probably smuggled in by Bonnie. He was soon recaptured and sent to the notorious Eastham Prison Farm, where he murdered a man who had sexually assaulted him. When he got out in February 1932, he reportedly vowed: 'I'll die before I go back to a place like that.'

The two of them and various accomplices began a spree of robberies. Bonnie was arrested after a burglary at the hardware store in Kaufman, Texas. She spent three months in jail before the charges were dropped due to insufficient evidence. Meanwhile Clyde had committed a number of hold-ups. During one at a jewellery store, the proprietor was killed, and he and an accomplice killed a sheriff and his deputy outside a barn dance in Oklahoma.

Reunited, Bonnie and Clyde were stopped driving a stolen car and took the sheriff prisoner, reportedly saying when they released him: 'Tell your people we ain't a bunch of nutty killers, sheriff, just down-home people tryin' to get through this damned Depression with a few bones.'

There followed a raid on the National Guard armoury in Abilene, Texas, where Clyde acquired his prized Browning automatic rifle, and hold-ups at a bank and a grocery store when the proprietor was killed. In Temple, Texas, they killed a man who tried to stop them stealing his car. Two weeks later a deputy was killed in a shoot-out.

In March 1933, Clyde's brother Buck, who was on parole, and his wife Blanche joined the gang. In April two detectives were killed in a violent shoot-out in Joplin, Missouri. The gang escaped in a stolen car, leaving behind Bonnie's poem 'Suicide Sal', and photographs of Bonnie brandishing a shotgun, chomping on a cigar and posing beside a stolen car.

They then travelled around the Midwest and southern states

robbing banks. In Ruston, Louisiana, they kidnapped an under-taker and his girlfriend while stealing his car, dropping them off in Arkansas. The man told reporters that, when she learnt his occupation, Bonnie had said: 'When the law catches us, you can fix us up.'

The town marshal of Alma, Texas, was killed after they had robbed a bank. In Platte City, Missouri, the motel where they were staying was raked by an armoured car and submachine guns. Surrounded in a deserted amusement park at Dexter, Iowa, Bonnie and Clyde escaped the withering fusillade, while Buck was mortally wounded and Blanche captured.

In January 1934, the fugitives attacked Eastham Prison Farm, freeing a handful of prisoners including Henry Methvin. During the raid, a prison officer was killed. The two were now 'Wanted Dead or Alive'; reward $2,500. Former Texas Ranger Frank Hamer was hired to hunt them down as the murders of state troopers and policemen continued.

Seeking to save his son from the death penalty, Methvin's father contacted Hamer. They arranged an ambush in Gibsland, Louisiana. When Bonnie and Clyde arrived, Hamer and his five-man posse riddled their car with 167 rounds, killing them instantly.

The story of Bonnie and Clyde

Also known as 'The Trail's End', this was the second of two poems Bonnie Parker wrote while on the run. She gave it to her mother just weeks before she and Clyde Barrow were gunned down.

> You've read the story of Jesse James
> Of how he lived and died;
> If you're still in need
> Of something to read,
> Here's the story of Bonnie and Clyde.
> Now Bonnie and Clyde are the Barrow gang,

I'm sure you all have read
How they rob and steal
And those who squeal
Are usually found dying or dead ...
If they try to act like citizens
And rent them a nice little flat,
About the third night
They're invited to fight
By a sub-gun's rat-tat-tat.
They don't think they're too tough or desperate,
They know that the law always wins;
They've been shot at before,
But they do not ignore
That death is the wages of sin.
Some day they'll go down together;
And they'll bury them side by side;
To few it'll be grief
To the law a relief
But it's death for Bonnie and Clyde.

MARIE ALEXANDRINE BECKER

Killer Cougar *Belgium, 1932–36*

Unusually for a serial killer, Marie Alexandrine Becker lived a blameless life until well into her fifties. Then the Liège housewife went on a spree of killing, stealing and forgery. Her motive seemed to be in part sexual. Her victims were killed for their money, which was then spent on a series of young lovers.

After twenty years of marriage, fifty-two-year-old Marie Becker began an affair with middle-aged rake Lambert Beyer, who picked her up when she was buying vegetables at a market stall. Her cabinetmaker husband stood in the way of this tempestuous romance, so she poisoned him. She tired of Beyer and he died too. Both left money to her.

Becker was now dancing wildly with men at the local nightclubs. Often she would pay young gigolos to escort her home and take her to bed. This was an expensive business and soon she was getting short of money.

While leading the high life at night, Becker had not neglected her friends, attending to them by day: when Marie Castadot fell ill, Becker offered to look after her. Her initial symptom of dizziness soon grew worse and she died. Becker nursed a number of other elderly friends who suffered the same fate.

'It seems that those who entrust themselves to your care have an undeviating tendency to die suddenly,' a magistrate said later.

'But they are old,' said Becker. 'What would you have? Is it not that everyone dies so, sooner or later?'

'That is true,' replied the magistrate. 'But also it is possible for the old to die before their time. I understand that you invariably served your patients tea, and justice demands that you inform me what you put into it.'

'Herbs,' said Becker. 'Only herbs of the most beneficent kinds. Herbs that would have healed them if it was that they were to live.'

It was discovered that the money she did not obtain by directly stealing from her victims, she got by forging their wills or obtained by fraud.

When she ran out of elderly friends, she began killing customers of a boutique she had invested in. Victims would be invited into a back room of the shop to discuss the latest fashions. There she would poison her victims by putting digitalis in a cup of tea or a glass of wine. She would then accompany them home, where she would take over as nurse with the same results as before.

Becker disposed of ten to twelve old ladies this way. She attended their funerals where she was seen dressed in black, kneeling at the graveside in tears. After leaving the cemetery, she would scurry off to spend their money on young men.

She was eventually caught when a friend, Madame Guichner, complained about her husband, saying: 'I wish he were dead.'

Becker replied: 'If you really mean that, I can supply you with a powder that will leave no trace.'

The police received an anonymous letter connecting her to the deaths of two victims. When the police visited her and searched her home, they found clothing, jewellery and other items belonging to her victims. They also found digitalis in her handbag.

'I suffered from heart trouble,' she explained, 'and I had to take it. I did not want my lover to know.'

But when doctors examined her they could find nothing wrong with her heart. As the judge later put it: 'In spite of your heart trouble you were known to go to dance halls and behave like a strong and flirtatious young woman. The druggist and chemist you name are dead, but the police have found no entries of your case in their registers.'

She spent nineteen months in prison, while the bodies of her victims were exhumed. Traces of digitalis were found in every single one. In court, Marie Becker was faced with ten lawyers, 1,800 items of evidence and 294 witnesses, every one of whose statements she contested.

'Everyone in the case is lying except you?' asked the judge.

'Yes,' she replied nodding vigorously.

Throughout she maintained the pose of an innocent woman who had been wronged by these accusations. She kept asking the judge to hurry as she had other matters to attend to. His response was that she had yet to clear herself. She was found guilty of eleven murders and sentenced to death. However, in Belgium, the death sentence is automatically commuted to life imprisonment. She died in jail in 1942.

Lost youth

One explanation for Becker's middle-aged murder spree is that she was trying to recapture her lost youth. It was reported that she appeared in court made up gaudily and dressed like a sixteen-year-old flapper. A dozen former teenage loves testified that she had lavished money and presents on them. She was forced to admit that this left her always in need of money. In her defence, she said: 'As for my going out with young people, my theory has always been that one is as young as one thinks oneself to be. As for what little money I spent on my friends from time to time, well, somehow Providence always saw to it that I was well cared for in worldly things. I seldom worried.'

ANNA MARIE HAHN

The Blonde Borgia *USA, 1933–37*

By the age of thirty-one, Anna Marie Hahn had murdered at least five elderly men in Cincinnati and Colorado with a variety of poisons, robbing them in the process to support her gambling habit. The beautiful coiffure and elegant attire in court earned her the sobriquet 'The Blonde Borgia' in the newspapers of the time.

Authorities in Colorado Springs began investigating a murder when doctors could not determine a cause of death when sixty-seven-year-old George Obendorfer mysteriously fell ill and died at the Memorial Hospital there on 1 August 1937.

Visiting from Cincinnati, Ohio, Obendorfer had been staying at the Park Hotel in Colorado Springs. Police discovered that it just so happened that Anna Hahn and her young son Oskar – also from Cincinnati – had also been staying at the hotel and suspicions were raised. Detectives then found that a woman answering Anna's description had been trying to sell missing jewels and withdraw $1,000 from a Denver bank using Obendorfer's bankbook.

When she was picked up back in Cincinnati, Anna Hahn at first claimed not to know Obendorfer. But according to Obendorfer's family, the couple had been travelling to Colorado together to visit a ranch she said she owned. Hahn then changed her story, insisting that she had only met Obendorfer on the train. Plainly the police had to look into her background.

Born Anna Marie Filser in Bavaria in 1906, she had an illegitimate child and was sent to the US in 1929. In Cincinnati, she met and married Phillip Hahn, returning to Germany briefly to collect her son. The marital home and the business they ran suffered a number of fires and the police suspected she was an arsonist.

In an effort to gain money, she tried to get her husband to take out a life insurance policy for $25,000. Even though he refused, he fell ill and, against Anna's wishes, his mother took him to hospital. He survived, but the marriage was over.

Detectives soon found that Anna Hahn was connected to another mysterious death they had been investigating – that of seventy-eight-year-old Jacob Wagner, who had left his entire estate to her. She had claimed to be his long-lost niece, though he had no living relatives. A lady in his apartment block had eaten an ice cream that Hahn had given her and became violently ill. While she was in hospital, money and jewellery were taken from her apartment.

Sixty-two-year-old George Heis then came forward, saying that he had been violently ill after Hahn had poured a beer for him. She had stolen from him, leading him to sack her as his carer. Weeks before she travelled to Colorado, she had gone to work for sixty-seven-year-old George Gsellman. He had also fallen ill and died shortly after her last visit. His body was found to contain a large amount of croton oil – a diarrhoea medicine that in large doses can kill. Phillip Hahn then handed over a bottle of croton oil that he had taken from his wife.

During a search of her house, the police found an IOU for $2,000. She had borrowed money from seventy-two-year-old Albert Palmer, who died while she was nursing him. She had kept the money and taken back the note. A further $4,000 was missing from his estate.

When her son Oskar was questioned, he contradicted his mother's story that they had met Obendorfer on the train. Rather she had bought his ticket at Union Terminal, Cincinnati, and she had given him several drinks on the train before he fell ill.

Instead of extraditing her back to Colorado, the authorities in Ohio decided to charge her with the murder of Jacob Wagner. In court, witnesses were called to testify about Wagner's agonizing end. A chemist said that he had found enough arsenic in his body to kill four men and a handwriting expert testified that Hahn had written Wagner's will.

Hahn took the stand in her own defence, but there was nothing she could do to refute the evidence against her. In his closing statement, the prosecutor said:

> She is sly, because she developed her relationships with old men who had no relatives and lived alone. She is avaricious, because no act was so low but that she was ready to commit it for slight gain. She is cold-blooded, like no other woman in the world, because no one could sit here for four weeks and hear this damaging parade of evidence and display no emotion. She is heartless, because nobody with a heart could deal out the death she dealt these old men. We've seen here the coldest, most heartless cruel person that ever has come within the scope of our lives. In the four corners of this courtroom stand four dead men. Gsellman, Palmer, Wagner, Obendorfer! From the four corners bony fingers point at her and say: 'That woman poisoned me! That woman made my last moments an agony! That woman tortured me with the tortures of the dammed!'

The jury took just two hours to reach their verdict – guilty with no recommendation for mercy. Asked whether she had anything to say before sentencing, she replied: 'I am innocent, your honour.'

She was sentenced to death by electrocution and taken to Ohio State Penitentiary where she was executed on 7 December 1938. Before she died, she handed four letters to her attorney. They contained her confession, which was sold to the *Cincinnati Enquirer* and the money put in trust for Oskar's education.

The confession

I don't know how I could have done the things I did in my life [Anna Hahn wrote]. Only God knows what came over me when I gave Albert Palmer, that first one, that poison that caused his death. Up in heaven there is a God who will judge. He will know and He will tell me how it came about? He will tell me what caused me to do the same things to Mr Wagner and the last one, Mr Obendorfer. I never knew myself afterwards, and I don't know now ...

Hahn met Palmer at the race track. She borrowed money from him. When she could not pay it back he 'wanted me to be his girl'. If she did not do what he wanted, he would get an attorney onto her.

God knows that I did not want to kill him, and I don't know what put such a thought in my head. I remembered that down in the cellar was some rat poison. Something in my mind kept saying to me, 'give him a little of this and he won't trouble you anymore'.

She claimed that she did not kill Wagner for his money. Only afterwards did she write his will. She also admitted killing George Gsellman and George Obendorfer, but did not give details.

I have written this confession with the full knowledge that death is near, and I only ask one favour and that is that my son should not be judged for the wrongs his mother may have done.

[signed] Anna Marie Hahn

Begs for mercy

Before she died Hahn also addressed the witnesses to her execution, pleading: 'Isn't there anybody who will help me? Is nobody going to help me?'

'I'm sorry, but we have to do it, Mrs Hahn,' replied the warden.

She beckoned to the chaplain, saying: 'Father, come close.'

But when he gripped her hand, she whispered between sobs: 'Be careful, father. You will be killed.'

LEONARDA CIANCIULLI

The Soap-Maker of Correggio *Italy, 1939–40*

In the early twentieth century, people in provincial Italy were super-
stitious. Leonarda Cianciulli believed that her marriage had been
cursed. Pregnant seventeen times, she had three miscarriages
and lost another ten children when they were young. So, when
her eldest surviving son Giuseppe was to join the Italian Army in
the run-up to the Second World War, she felt she needed human
sacrifice to protect him.

L eonarda had a troubled childhood in the small town of
Montello in southern Italy. Born after her alcoholic father
had kidnapped and raped her mother, Leonarda attempted
suicide twice during her early years and the relationship between
mother and daughter was problematic.

Further troubles in life were portended when a gypsy told her:
'You will marry and have children, but all your children will die.'
Later another gypsy palm-reader told her: 'In your right hand I
see prison, in your left a criminal asylum.'

When Raffaele Pansardi, a registry clerk from Lauria, seventy
miles away, asked twenty-three-year-old Leonarda to marry him
in 1917, her mother cursed the union. Nevertheless, Leonarda
married and moved to Lauria. This brought her no luck. Her
husband was also an alcoholic and she went to prison for
fraud.

After she was released, they moved to Lacedonia. Bad luck
dogged her there too and their house was destroyed by an earth-
quake in 1930. Next, they moved to Correggio where Leonarda

ran a small shop to support herself and her four surviving children after her husband left her.

In 1935, Italy, under the Fascist dictator Benito Mussolini, invaded Abyssinia. This brought him into a pact with Hitler. Italy then invaded Albania and, as war loomed, Leonarda's favourite son Giuseppe was conscripted. She then fixed on her plan of human sacrifice.

Leonarda was also known as a poet and a fortune-teller herself and three of her friends turned to her for help. The first victim was fifty-year-old spinster Faustina Setti, who wanted to marry. She gave her 30,000-lire savings to Leonarda who said she had found her a husband, sixty miles away in Pola. After persuading Faustina to write letters and postcards to relatives explaining her marriage plans, Leonarda gave her drugged wine and killed her with an axe. She then chopped the body up into nine pieces, collecting the blood. The body was then dissolved in caustic soda to make soap and a candle, while the blood was used to make cakes, also using Faustina's ground bones as flour.

The second victim was fifty-three-year-old Francesca Clementina Soavi. She was an educated woman and Leonarda said that she had found her a job as a teacher in a girls' school in Piacenza, some sixty miles away, for a 3,000-lire fee. Again, Leonarda instructed her victim to write postcards to explain her plans. On the morning of 5 September 1940, Francesca dropped in to say goodbye to Leonarda and got no further.

The third victim was former opera singer Virginia Cacioppo, who was said to have sung *Madame Butterfly* at La Scala. At sixty, her singing career was long behind her and she, too, needed a job. Leonarda said she had found one for her as a secretary to a theatre impresario in Florence.

'The diva yielded 50,000 lire and assorted diamonds and rubies, as well as soap and candles,' said *Time* magazine.

However, Virginia's sister-in-law grew suspicious about her sudden disappearance. She told the police that Virginia had last been seen entering Leonarda Cianciulli's house. Her soap-making equipment was examined and, under questioning, she admitted the three murders. In 1946, she was sentenced to thirty years in prison, dying in the women's criminal asylum in Pozzuoli in 1970.

Confession

While awaiting trial, Cianciulli wrote an account of her crimes called *Confessions of an Embittered Soul*. In it, she described the murder of one friend: 'While my victim was drinking an elixir I had prepared, I got an axe, placed myself behind my victim and, summoning my strength, struck the back of her neck – a rattle, nothing else. It was a master stroke that almost beheaded her.'

Of disposing of Faustina Setti's body she said in her statement: 'I threw the pieces into a pot, added seven kilos of caustic soda, which I had bought to make soap, and stirred the whole mixture until the pieces dissolved in a thick, dark mush that I poured into several buckets and emptied in a nearby septic tank. As for the blood in the basin, I waited until it had coagulated, dried it in the oven, ground it and mixed it with flour, sugar, chocolate, milk and eggs, as well as a bit of margarine, kneading all the ingredients together. I made lots of crunchy tea cakes and served them to the ladies who came to visit, though Giuseppe and I also ate them.'

She said of Virginia Cacioppo: 'She ended up in the pot, like the other two . . . her flesh was fat and white; when it had melted I added a bottle of cologne, and after a long time on the boil I was able to make some most acceptable creamy soap. I gave bars to neighbours and acquaintances. The cakes, too, were better: that woman was really sweet.'

But she was nothing if not patriotic. She told the judge: 'I gave the copper ladle, which I used to skim the fat off the kettles, to my country, which was so badly in need of metal during the last days of the war.'

FLORENCE RANSOM

Glamorous Shotgun Assassin *England, 1940*

Attractive thirty-four-year-old widow Florence Ransom left her
home in Piddington, Oxfordshire, on 9 July 1940, and took the
8.56 a.m. train from Bicester. She was carrying a .410 sporting
shotgun she had borrowed from her brother, saying she was going
to shoot rabbits. Instead she travelled to Matfield in Kent. There
she shot Dorothy Sanders Fisher, her lover's forty-six-year-old
wife, his twenty-year-old daughter Freda Ann and their forty-eight-
year-old maid, Miss Charlotte Saunders.

It was Mrs Dorothy Fisher's custom to take tea on Tuesdays with
her eighty-three-year-old mother Mrs Gibbs. When she did not
turn up, Mrs Gibbs's housekeeper phoned Mrs Fisher's home,
but got no reply.

Mrs Gibbs sent her gardener to investigate. He found the body
of the family's maid Miss Saunders in the front garden. She had
sustained terrible head injuries. He called the police. A large squad
under Superintendent Cook arrived to make what investigations
they could before it got dark. In the orchard nearby, they found
the bodies of Mrs Fisher and her daughter Freda. The police
worked on the assumption that they had been shot first and, on
hearing the shots, the maid ran out of the door of the house only
to be struck down either by the butt of the gun or some other
instrument. A search of the grounds was made.

The following morning Scotland Yard's flying squad was on
the scene. The house was in disorder, but nothing valuable was
missing. A pond was dragged and the surrounding woodland

combed. In these searches was found a white ox-skin glove. It belonged to Florence Ransom.

THE FISHERS' AFFAIRS

Lawrence Fisher first met Florence Ransom, a red-headed beauty then aged twenty-eight, in 1934. Dorothy Fisher also took a lover of her own. Both Mr and Mrs Fisher knew of each other's relationships. The arrangement seemed a perfectly civilized one and they continued to live together in Twickenham until the war. Then Lawrence moved in with Florence in Oxfordshire, while Dorothy and her daughter moved to Kent.

However, when the Battle of Britain started, Kent found itself in the front line. Mr Fisher travelled down to Matfield frequently to make sure that his wife and daughter were safe. He also gave them money so they could employ a serving maid. This, apparently, made Mrs Ransom jealous.

Mrs Ransom claimed that she stayed at the farm in Piddington all day on 9 July. However, a week earlier, she had bought twenty-five .410 cartridges in Oxford and her brother had taught her how to shoot. She had also been seen on the train, carrying a brown paper package which the prosecution maintained contained the gun. They also alleged that she had maintained the story that she had gone out shooting rabbits with Freda Fisher. Walking out into the orchard, Mrs Ransom shot the young woman in the back at close range. Dorothy Fisher saw what had happened and fled, but Ransom chased after her and shot her in the back twice. She then went back to finish off Freda with two more shots. Her glove was found near the bodies; it was thought that she had taken it off while reloading.

Back at the cottage, Charlotte Saunders was making tea. When Ransom returned to the house, she fled and Ransom shot her in the head. The sound of shots would not have drawn any attention. At the time, Britain was expecting a Nazi invasion and Kent was full of soldiers in training.

Mrs Ransom had a record of mental instability and had been a voluntary patient on several occasions. However, during her trial in November 1940, she underwent prolonged cross-examination without turning a hair. She was convicted and sentenced to death. Afterwards, though, she was found to be insane and sent to Broadmoor.

MARGARET 'BILL' ALLEN

Transgender Hammer Murderer *England, 1948*

Margaret Allen claimed to have had a sex-change operation in 1935, when she was twenty-nine, though the procedure was first carried out in 1946. Calling herself Bill, she cut her hair short, wore men's clothes, took on labouring jobs, traditionally the preserve of men, and hung out with men in pubs and working-men's clubs of her hometown Rawtenstall, Lancashire. Then a local skinflint named Nancy Chadwick was found dead in the street. Three days later Allen was arrested for her murder.

The twentieth of twenty-two children, Allen loaded coal, repaired houses and, during the Second World War, became a bus conductor. Her mother's death in 1943 badly affected her, and she became withdrawn and depressed. She had one friend in the world, Mrs Annie Cook, who rejected her advances. By 1945, Allen was being treated by a doctor for bouts of dizziness and in 1946 she lost her job on the buses for abusing passengers.

She had invested her savings, buying a rundown home that had once been a police cottage. The place was infested with lice and even the gas cooker had been sold to pay the bills. According to Mrs Cook, she had twice tried to kill herself, having become increasingly lonely.

At about 3.35 a.m. 29 August 1948, the body of sixty-eight-year-old Nancy Ellen Chadwick was spotted by bus driver Herbert Beaumont at the side of the road by Rawtenstall's main street, a few feet from Allen's home. Another bus driver, Arthur Marshall, told police the body had not been there when he had passed fifteen minutes earlier. The victim's coat had been pulled up, hiding extensive head injuries. At first she appeared to be a hit-and-run victim, but a post-mortem carried out by Dr Gilbert Bailey of Blackburn determined that her wounds had been made with the pointed end of a hammer used to break up coal. She had been battered to death. Local paper the *Bacup Times* reported that it was the first murder in Rawenstall in living memory.

Allen began to take an inordinate interest in the investigation of Chadwick's murder. When the police searched the area, Allen pointed out Chadwick's bag floating in the River Irwell nearby. Mrs Chadwick had been known to always carry large amounts of money in her bag, but when they recovered it, there was no money at all inside.

Allen also boasted in pubs that she had been the last person to see Chadwick, roundly condemning her for sitting on a road bench counting her money. Naturally, the police went to Allen's house to interview her. They found blood on the walls and inside the front door. Allen freely confessed the murder.

'I'll tell you all about it,' she said, leading them to the coal cellar. 'That's where I put her. I didn't actually do it for the money. I was in one of my funny moods.'

Chadwick was a neighbour and the two women had never got on. The dispute that day seems to have been about sugar, which was still rationed at the time. After killing Chadwick, Allen left her body in the coal cellar and threw her bag and the hammer in the Irwell river. Then she went to have a drink with Mrs Cook. She returned to the pub that evening. During the night, she decided to dispose of the corpse in the river, but it was too heavy to drag that far, so she abandoned it in the street.

Margaret Allen's trial lasted just five hours. Allen wore a man's suit in the dock, which did her no favours with the court at the time. The defence was insanity, given her confession did not hold water. The jury took just ten minutes to find her guilty and the judge passed a sentence of death. Mrs Cook made an attempt to get up a petition for a reprieve. It was signed by just 162 people. While the Home Secretary James Chuter Ede was personally opposed to the death penalty, he could find no grounds to commute the sentence and Allen did not appeal.

When Mrs Cook visited her for the last time before she was hanged, Allen said: 'I'm going to have chicken for dinner and a few bottles before they put the rope around my neck. It would help if I could cry, but my manhood holds back my tears.'

Mrs Cook told the press: 'I don't think Allen ever realized the seriousness of her position. She seemed to have nerves of iron.'

In fact, her last meal was a plate of scrambled eggs. She refused to eat them and, kicking over the tray, said: 'I don't want it and no one else is going to enjoy it.'

She was hanged by public executioner Albert Pierrepoint in Strangeways jail in Manchester on 12 January 1949. Allen was not allowed to wear men's clothing for the execution and was given a striped prison dress instead.

The Reverend Arthur Walker, the chaplain at Strangeways, witnessed the event. He said: 'She was a woman with plenty of grit and she faced it as a man would and I felt the whole thing was bestial and brutal. She was well prepared and behaved like a man. In fact she had more guts than most men I have seen. A prison official has told me that he has never felt fit since the thing happened and it happened over twelve months ago.'

He told a Royal Commission on capital punishment the following year that no woman should be hanged. 'If the state recognised the physical and mental differences between the sexes and refused to flog women then the more cruel punishment of hanging should be abolished,' he said.

RHONDA BELLE MARTIN

Little Mrs Arsenic *USA, 1937–51*

In 1956, a forty-nine-year-old waitress in Montgomery, Alabama, named Rhonda Belle Martin admitted murdering her mother, two husbands and three of her children. She also admitted the attempted murder of her fifth husband, who was formerly her stepson. Although she had taken out insurance on all her victims, the amounts were trivial and even she could not find any reason for her crimes.

Rhonda Gipson, née Thomley, married Claude C. Martin in 1950. A year after they were married, he became gravely ill, suffering severe abdominal pain and vomiting frequently. Doctors thought it was a virus, but there was nothing they could do for him and, after several weeks of intense pain, he died.

Eight months after Claude's death, Mrs Martin married her stepson Ronald C. Martin, twenty-one years her junior. Whether this union was incestuous was argued over later in court. However, after four years of marriage, Ronald began to suffer from the same mysterious illness that had killed his father and, after a year, he became paralysed from the waist down. In an attempt to find a diagnosis, doctors took a sample of his hair to analyse and found arsenic.

The police then began to investigate Rhonda's background and found that those around her died with astonishing frequency. Her second husband George Garrett had died, ostensibly of pneumonia, in 1937. That same year, their three-year-old daughter Emogene died, along with Rhonda's mother, Mary F. Gibbon.

Three years later six-year-old Ann Carolyn Garrett died. Then in 1943, eleven-year-old Ellyn Elizabeth Garrett died, supposedly of a 'stomach ailment'. Rhonda admitted killing all five. Along the way, two other daughters – Mary Adelaide and Judith – also died, but Rhonda denied killing them.

In 1939, Rhonda had married Talmadge John Gipson, but they swiftly divorced and he got away with his life. Then Rhonda met and married Claude Martin, a widower with three daughters and one son. When he died, Rhonda collected a $2,750 insurance payment, using $400 of it to have the body of Claude's first wife moved so they could be together.

Rhonda's marriage to Claude's son Ronald was happy enough, but that may be because he was away at sea a lot. But after he was discharged from the Navy in 1955, he fell ill. This sparked the investigation that led to the exhumation of the other bodies. Large quantities of arsenic were found in those of her mother, children and husbands.

After three days of questioning, Rhonda signed a statement admitting killing six and poisoning Ronald. She was tried only for the murder of her fourth husband, Claude C. Martin. Her plea of insanity failed with the prosecution arguing that she had deliberately put arsenic in her husband's coffee to 'collect some paltry amount of insurance and to get him out of the way so she could marry his son'. She was convicted and sentenced to death.

Under Alabama's state law, the conviction automatically went to appeal at the state's Supreme Court. There it was argued that Rhonda's confession was inadmissible because, in it, she had also admitted to marrying her stepson. As this was incestuous, she was admitting a felony which was not part of the issue being tried, so could not be used in evidence. But the Supreme Court judged that, as Claude Martin was dead at the time of Rhonda's marriage to Ronald – and she and Martin Sr had no children – the marriage was not incestuous, so she was not admitting a crime and the confession was consequently admissible.

This dashed Rhonda's hope for a retrial. It was also clear that the sentence would not be commuted to life imprisonment. After a last meal of hamburger, mashed potatoes, cinnamon roll and coffee, she walked into the death chamber wearing a new dress she had made and her wedding ring. At seven minutes after midnight on 11 October 1956, she was strapped into the electric chair and asked if she had anything to say. She shook her head. The switch was then thrown, but it was found that the electrodes had not been plugged into the chair. Three minutes later, she was given 2,200 volts of electricity and, soon after, pronounced dead.

Later, a note was found in her Bible which read: 'At my death, whether it be a natural death or otherwise, I want my body to be given to some scientific institution to be used as they see fit, but especially to see if someone can find out why I committed the crimes I have committed. I can't understand it, for I had no reason whatsoever. There is definitely something wrong. Can't someone find it and save someone else the agony I have been through.'

The confession

In the controversial confession signed by Rhonda Belle Martin she admitted putting poison in her husband's coffee over a period of several months preceding and during his fatal illness. This was not disputed and from the record it clearly appeared that the confession was voluntary. The confession was made in the form of questions and answers and contained the following references to the defendant's marriage to her husband's son:

Q. Did he [the deceased] have an automobile?
A. Yes sir.
Q. Was there any kind of insurance policy on that automobile that it paid up at his death?
A. Yes sir.
Q. What kind? What kind of automobile was it?

A. A '49 Hudson.

Q. Did you inherit anything else from him?

A. No sir. I don't think there was anything else.

Q. When did you start going with his son?

A. Well, it was three or four months after he died.

Q. Did his son live with him?

A. He was in the Navy.

Q. In the Navy the whole time you were married?

A. Yes sir.

Q. When did he get out? When was he discharged?

A. This February two years ago.

Q. He was in the Navy when you married him?

A. Yes sir.

Q. Where did you move after Mr Martin died? Claude Martin died?

A. 519 Montgomery Street.

Q. Did he own any real estate?

A. No sir.

Q. You gave him three or four more doses? And the last dose was two or three weeks before he died?

A. No sir, longer than that, a month or more before he died.

Q. After Mr Martin's death, you married his son?

A. Yes sir.

Q. How long after?

A. December 7, 1951, that would have been how long after his death.

Q. How long after Mr Martin's death?

A. He died in April, about eight months, I guess.

CAROLINE GRILLS

Aunt Thally *Australia, 1947–53*

In Sydney, Australia, in the 1950s, Aunt Carrie often visited relatives and friends and liked to make tea, cake and biscuits for them. After these visits they became very ill, suffering hair loss, nervous disorders, progressive blindness, loss of speech and in some cases death – all symptoms of thallium poisoning. She was eventually charged with four murders and three attempted murders.

Caroline Grills' sister-in-law Eveline Lundberg and Lundberg's daughter Christine Downing became ill each time Aunt Carrie visited. Christine's husband John also suffered. One day he saw Grills reach into her dress pocket and drop something in the cup of tea she was carrying. He managed to divert her attention and pour some of the tea into a bottle. He took this to the police who tested it and discovered that it contained the poison thallium.

On 11 May 1953, Caroline Grills was charged with the attempted murder of Mrs Lundberg and Mrs Downey. The police then began to investigate the high mortality rate among Grills' circle. This led them to charge Grills with four murders and one more attempted murder. All of the victims, with the exception of a friend of her mother's, were in-laws.

Grills' killing spree seems to have begun in November 1947 with the murder of her eighty-seven-year-old stepmother Christina Mickelson. Another suspected victim was Angelina Thomas, a relation of her husband's who died in January 1948. The coroner also held Grills responsible for the deaths of her sister-in-law Mary Anne Michelson and John Lundberg, another relative by marriage, after two of the bodies of suspected victims were unearthed and thallium was found in them. The others had been cremated, so no tests could be made. However, at the coroner's inquest, witnesses reported Grills bringing the deceased drinks and always being eager to supply them tea and cakes.

While the police had strong circumstantial evidence to support these charges, they only proceeded with the single charge of attempting to murder Mrs Lundberg, who described how her hair had fallen out and she had slowly lost her sight. John Downey said that he had become suspicious after reading a report of another thallium murder in a newspaper in October 1952.

In court, Senior Crown Prosecutor Mick Rooney, QC, described Grills as 'a killer who poisoned for sport, for fun, for the kicks she got out of it, for the hell of it, for the thrill that she and she alone in the world knew the cause of the victims' suffering'. Grills protested her innocence, insisting that the police had pressured her relatives into giving evidence against her. However, her outbursts of laughter in court reinforced the idea that she was a malicious killer. The jury took just twelve minutes to convict. On hearing the verdict, she said: 'I helped to live, not to kill.'

Thallium was banned soon after.

Her appeal was dismissed by the Court of Criminal Appeal in April 1954, but her sentence was commuted to life imprisonment. She was admitted to the State Reformatory for Women where she spent the next six-and-a-half years. There Aunt Carrie was known as Aunt Thally.

On 6 October 1960, she was rushed to Prince Henry Hospital where she died from peritonitis from a ruptured gastric ulcer and her body was cremated. It remained a puzzle why this matronly figure with thick-rimmed glasses turned to murder in her sixties – or why she took against her in-laws. She was survived by her husband, Richard Grills, a daughter and three sons.

Australia's 'Thallium Craze'

There was a spate of murders using thallium in Australia in the early 1950s, when thallium sulphate was used as a rat poison and was sold over the counter in New South Wales. From March 1952 until the arrest of Grills there had been forty-six cases of reported thallium poisoning, involving ten deaths. The first case to make the headlines was in September 1952 when Sydney housewife Yvonne Gladys Fletcher used thallium to kill her abusive second husband, Bertrand 'Bluey' Fletcher, a rat-bait layer who used the poison in his work. The fact that he exhibited the same symptoms as her first husband, Desmond Butler, who died in 1948, raised enough suspicion for his body to be exhumed. It was found to contain thallium. The judge found she had a "black hatred" of Butler and sentenced her to death, although this was commuted to life imprisonment when capital punished was abolished in New South Wales. She was released in 1964.

In October 1952, Ruby Norton stood trial after being charged with murdering her daughter's fiancé Allen Williams, who died of thallium poisoning in hospital that July. She was later acquitted, however, despite allegations that Norton hated all the men in her family and Williams was an unwanted son-in-law.

In July 1953, Beryl Hague was found guilty of 'maliciously administering thallium and endangering her husband's life'. She admitted to putting the rodent-poison Thall-rat in her husband's tea, though she claimed that she had not intended to kill him, only to give him a headache for all the headaches he had given her.

After the trial of Caroline Grills in October, Veronica Monty was tried for the attempted murder of her son-in-law, rugby league star Bobby Lulham who was treated for thallium poisoning in 1952. The couple had enjoyed an intimate relationship while her daughter was out at mass. Monty killed herself with thallium in 1955.

NANNIE DOSS

The Giggling Grandma *USA, 1924–54*

After the autopsy of her fifth husband revealed he had enough arsenic in him to kill twenty men, forty-nine-year-old Nannie Doss giggled under interrogation as she admitted killing him and three previous husbands. It is likely that she also killed her mother, her mother-in-law, her sister, two of her children and two grandchildren along the way. Although she collected insurance money on the deceased, Doss claimed that she murdered for love. Her head had been turned by true romance magazines and love stories on the TV, and she said she killed those who got in the way of her search for the perfect mate.

Born in 1905 in the Blue Mountains of Alabama and one of five children, Nancy Hazle was nicknamed Nannie as a child. She had little schooling as her father insisted on the children helping on the farm and the reading material available there consisted solely of her mother's collection of true romance magazines. After a train accident where she hit her head, she suffered headaches and blackouts, and she would later blame her mental instability on the incident.

Her father was extremely strict and would not let his daughters wear make-up or attractive clothing, or go to dances. When she was fifteen, her father gave his permission for her to marry Charlie Braggs, whom she had met at the Linen Thread Company factory where they worked, as Braggs supported his unmarried mother and, therefore, respected his elders.

Nannie moved in with Braggs and his mother, whom she soon

discovered was as much of a tyrant as her father. They had four daughters, but Braggs became an alcoholic and a womanizer and was rarely home. Nannie began drinking and smoking too, and rivalled her husband in the number of lovers she accumulated.

One day in early 1927, Braggs returned home to find his two middle daughters dead, ostensibly of food poisoning. His mother also died around this time. Braggs took fright and fled. The couple divorced in 1929.

Nannie had already begun to look for a new husband in the lonely hearts columns. She found a good-looking twenty-three-year-old factory worker from Jackson, Alabama, named Frank Harrelson, and they married. But she soon found that he, too, was an alcoholic, and even worse, he had been convicted of assault and spent time in jail. Nevertheless the marriage lasted sixteen years.

When Nannie's eldest daughter Melvina was having trouble giving birth to her second child, her husband called for her help. The child died soon after birth. Melvina thought she saw her mother stab the child in the head with a hat pin. Six months later, Melvina's son Robert also passed away while in Nannie's care.

One night, roaring drunk, Harrelson demanded sex. She refused. After he had taken what he wanted anyway, her retaliation was swift and fatal.

'I went and got the whiskey bottle out of the flour bin in the kitchen and poured poison into it, I thought I'll just teach him a lesson,' she told the police later. Harrelson died a painful death soon after.

Nannie returned to the lonely hearts columns and found a new husband, Arlie J. Lanning. She poisoned him, she said, because he was 'running around with other women'. A nephew living with them died of 'food poisoning', while his elderly mother also died soon after. The house also burned down, rendering more insurance money.

Nannie went to take care of her sister Dovie who was bed-ridden. She died soon after. Nannie's seventy-three-year-old mother also died under her care. At a singles' club, she met Richard L. Morton. He too was a womanizer, so Nannie put an end to him.

Next came church-going Samuel L. Doss who disapproved of Nannie reading the true romance stories she loved, listening to the radio or visiting friends to watch television. She laced his stewed prunes with arsenic and he ended up in hospital, where he recovered. However, the night he went home, she finished him off with a large dose of arsenic in his coffee. The sudden death alerted his doctor, who requested a post-mortem.

Belated autopsies on her sister and mother also revealed arsenic. Investigators also looked into the deaths of two other sisters who both died in 1953, but Nannie denied killing them.

On 18 May 1955, in Tulsa, Oklahoma, Nannie Doss pleaded guilty to the murder of Samuel Doss and was sentenced to life in prison. She did not face other murder charges as they had happened in other states.

Good-humoured to the end, Nannie told a reporter who visited her in prison: 'When they get shorthanded in the kitchen here, I always offer to help out, but they never let me.'

A model prisoner, she died of leukemia on 2 June 1965, aged fifty-nine.

RUTH ELLIS

Last Woman to Be Hanged in the UK
England, 1955

On 10 April 1955, popular nightclub hostess Ruth Ellis pulled a gun from her handbag and shot her lover David Blakely outside The Magdala pub in Hampstead. There was no doubt about that, but her barrister argued that, because of the provocation she had suffered, she should only be found guilty of manslaughter. She did not help his case. A striking figure in the witness box with her bleached-blonde hair, she admitted that she had meant to kill him. Convicted of murder, she refused to appeal and went bravely to the gallows just three months after the crime.

Ruth Ellis, née Neilson, was born in Rhyl in 1926. She and her elder sister Muriel were abused by her father. Eager to get away from home, it became plain to Ruth that her passport to a better life was her good looks. She pinned her hopes on a Canadian serviceman, who she discovered to have a wife and two children back home. They broke up, but soon after, eighteen-year-old Ruth gave birth to a son.

After a series of menial jobs, Ruth became a photographic model, then a hostess in various clubs in Mayfair. She briefly left the work when she married George Johnston Ellis, but the marriage failed by the time she gave birth to a daughter, and she soon returned to Mayfair as a hostess and part-time escort.

SINISTER CONNECTIONS

There are indications that she moved in the same circles as celebrity osteopath Stephen Ward, who later introduced model and showgirl Christine Keeler to Soviet military attaché Yevgney Ivanov and British secretary of state for war John Profumo, resulting in a scandal known as the Profumo Affair which rocked the Conservative government in 1963. While helping Muriel Jakubait write *Ruth Ellis: My Sister's Secret Life*, co-author Monica Well also unearthed Ruth's connections to Kim Philby and the Cambridge spy ring, but the files in the National Archives are closed until 2031.

She became manageress of The Little Club in Knightsbridge, living in the flat above. There she met racing driver David Blakely. Although he was engaged to another woman, they became lovers and he moved in with her. However, his heavy drinking and jealousy caused trouble at the club. While he took other lovers, she took up with Desmond Cussen, a former bomber pilot and director of the family retail chain of tobacconists. The fights between Blakely and Ellis grew more frequent. As a result she lost her job and the flat that went with it. In one tussle, Blakely punched her in the stomach and she miscarried.

Ten days later, on 10 April 1955, carrying a gun she initially said had been given to her by an American soldier as security on a loan, she went to 29 Tanza Road in Hampstead where she was convinced Blakely was visiting a mistress. Spurred on by drink, tranquillizers, pathological jealousy and three sleepless nights, she was determined to take her revenge. She saw his car parked outside the nearby Magdala pub. When Blakely came out, she pulled the gun and pumped four bullets into him, one at a distance of less than three inches. A bystander, Mrs Gladys Yule, was wounded in the hand by a stray bullet. When a policeman approached, Ellis said: 'Arrest me. I have just shot this man. And call an ambulance.'

Once she was in custody, she said: 'I'm guilty. I'm rather confused. When I put the gun into my bag I intended to go and find David and shoot him. I thought I had missed him so I fired again. He was still running so I fired a third shot. I don't remember firing any more, but I must have done.'

Formally charge with murder at Hampstead magistrates' court, she said: 'An eye for an eye, a tooth for a tooth. I will hang.' And she refused her solicitor's attempt to enter a plea of insanity.

'I took David's life and I don't ask you to save mine,' she said. 'I don't want to live.'

Although Ellis pleaded not guilty, she did nothing to dispel the impression the witnesses gave of a cold-blooded murder. Even her bleached-blonde hair and chic black suit spoke of the heartless femme fatale beloved of pulp fiction. When asked by the prosecution what she had intended to do when she fired at close range into Blakely's body, she said: 'It's obvious. When I shot him, I intended to kill him.'

On the strength of that admission, the judge ruled that the jury could not find her guilty of the lesser charge of manslaughter. The trial lasted less than two days. In his summing up, Justice Havers said that her defence was 'so weak . . . it was non-existent'. After half an hour of consideration, the jury found her guilty of murder. Then the judge pronounced the sentence of death.

Ruth was sanguine. She told her mother: 'I was sane when I did it, and I meant to do it. I won't go to prison for ten years or more and come out old and finished.'

Nevertheless a petition was created asking for clemency, which was signed by fifty thousand people.

Throughout the proceedings, Ellis had shielded her lover Cussen's involvement. But on the day before she faced execution, her lawyer Victor Mishcon persuaded her to make a last statement, detailing his complicity. This was sent on to the home secretary, Major Gwilym Lloyd George. But Cussen could not be found and the home secretary found no grounds to reprieve her, reasoning you could not have people shooting off firearms in the street as a passer-by was also injured.

A crowd of more than five hundred gathered outside the gates of Holloway prison on the morning of the execution. Despite public protests, the hangman Albert Pierrepoint despatched her at 9 a.m. on 13 July 1955.

'I have seen some brave men die, but nobody braver than her,' he said.

She was buried, as required by law, within the walls of Holloway prison, but much later exhumed and reburied in the graveyard of St Mary's Church in Amersham, Buckinghamshire.

ABOLITION OF THE DEATH PENALTY

The public revulsion at the execution of a twenty-eight-year-old woman expedited the establishment of the defence of 'diminished responsibility' in the Homicide Act of 1957. Ten years after Ruth's execution, the Murder (Abolition of the Death Penalty) Act was passed, suspending capital punishment, and in 1969 it was permanently abolished.

DELFINA AND MARÍA DE JESÚS GONZÁLEZ

The Madams from Hell *Mexico, 1950s–63*

Delfina and María de Jesús González ran Rancho Loma del Ángel, also known as the 'bordello from hell'. The girls there were forced into prostitution. Once they had lost their looks or if they failed to satisfy clients, they were murdered. Men who brought too much money to the bordello were also killed and their money stolen. The González sisters killed around 110 people, making them the 'most prolific murder partnership', according to Guinness World Records.

The González sisters recruited girls by putting small ads in local papers asking for maids. If the girls were attractive enough they would be promised good pay and a home from home. Then they would either be sold on to other madams at $40 to $80, or put to work in their own brothels. Those who resisted were beaten and tortured. They either worked or died. To make them more compliant they were forced into cocaine or heroin addiction.

Girls who got pregnant were forced to have an abortion. One who refused was hung up by the hands and beaten around the body until she miscarried. They were fed only tortillas and beans. After about five years, most girls were no longer attractive and were killed. Contracting a sexually transmitted disease was also a death sentence. Victims would be beaten or starved to death. Bodies were dumped in mass graves, or sometimes in shallow graves where they were exhumed later and burnt. They were joined in their graves by aborted foetuses and rich punters who had been robbed.

As the business expanded, the sisters hired Hermenegildo 'The Black Eagle' Zuniga and Estrada 'The Executioner' Bocanegra to kidnap new girls. Virgins were particularly prized and clients were willing to pay top dollar for them. Delfina's son Ramon 'El Tepo' Torres was also on hand to maintain discipline. The girls were never allowed out. Inmates compared Rancho Loma del Ángel to a concentration camp.

BACKGROUND

Delfina, María de Jesús, Carmen and María Luisa González Valenzuela were born to poverty in El Salto de Juanacatlan, Jalisco, in western Mexico in the 1910s. Their father Isidro Torres was a policeman and was not above throwing his daughters in jail for wearing make-up, sexy clothing or having boyfriends he did not approve of. After shooting a man in an argument, he took his family to live in the small village of San Francisco del Rincon, called San Pancho by the locals, in the neighbouring state of Guanajuato.

To escape their authoritarian father, the sisters opened a bar. When this was not a success, they moved into prostitution, running a chain of bar-cum-brothels in Jalisco, Guanajuato and Queretaro states. Offering bribes and sexual services to the authorities, they managed to operate with impunity. One of their establishments was a saloon purchased from a gay man called 'El Poquianchi' and the name Poquianchis stuck.

Accounts of how their operation came to an end differ. In one version, in 1963, El Tepo got into an argument with a policeman, who shot El Tepo dead inside one of the brothels. The police closed down the place and it was said that Delfina, El Tepo's mother, ordered Hermenegildo Zuniga to track down the cop who killed her son and kill him. In the ensuing enquiry, the police picked up a procuress named Josefina Gutiérrez on suspicion of kidnapping young girls in the Guanajuato area. During questioning, she implicated the two sisters.

In another version, three inmates of Rancho Loma del Ángel managed to escape. One of them, Catalina Ortega, managed to find her way back to her mother, who took her to the police station in the city of Leon, Guanajuato, to file a complaint. They were in luck – the policeman was not on the sisters' payroll. Catalina's story was substantiated by clear signs of abuse and malnutrition.

On 14 January 1964, the Rancho Loma del Ángel was raided. Zuniga was one of those forced to excavate the graves. The bodies of eighty women, eleven men and an unknown number of infants and foetuses were found. Delfina and María fled but were caught selling their possessions ready to skip the country.

The sisters denied any wrongdoing. Delfina insisted: 'The little dead ones died all by themselves ... Maybe the food did not agree with them.'

Another sister, María Luisa González, aka 'Eva the Leggy One', ran a separate operation but, fearing that she may be lynched, turned herself in in Mexico City. A fourth sister, Carmen, had already died of cancer.

As well as being charged with rape, murder and extortion, the three sisters were also charged with corrupting and bribing the government officials who frequented their bars and brothels. In a chaotic trial, the sisters exchanged insults at the top of their voices. They were convicted and sentenced to forty years in jail, the maximum sentence in Mexico.

Terrified that she would be murdered in jail, Delfina went mad and was killed in an accident when a workman making repairs above her cell dropped a bucket of cement on her head. María Luisa died alone in her cell after twenty years in jail on

19 November 1984. María de Jesús, the youngest of the sisters, was eventually released and died of old age in the 1990s.

In 2002, workers excavating the land for a new housing development in Purisima del Rincon, Guanajuato, near the notorious Loma del Ángel ranch, found around twenty skeletons in a pit. Authorities concluded that these belonged to other victims of the women known as Las Poquianchis. This would bring the death toll up to over 110.

MYRA HINDLEY

Moors Murderer *England, 1963–65*

Dubbed the most evil woman in Britain by the press, Myra Hindley, with her partner Ian Brady, murdered five children. They were known as the 'Moors Murderers', as they buried their victims' bodies on Saddleworth Moor in the Peak District, overlooking Manchester. The crime shocked the nation and the world, and Hindley became the very image of a depraved killer.

Even before she met Ian Brady, Myra Hindley had problems. Her father, a former paratrooper, beat her and had taught her to be tough and stick up for herself. She was also known as a loner and a daydreamer. At thirteen, a boyfriend invited her to go swimming in a nearby reservoir. She refused. When he drowned, she blamed herself. She could not sleep for days afterwards and eventually turned to the Catholic Church for consolation. At school it was noted that she was tough and aggressive, enjoying contact sports and judo. After school she had a series of menial jobs, before becoming a typist at Millwards, a wholesale chemical distribution company in Manchester. There she met Brady who already had a criminal record for housebreaking and threatening a girlfriend with a knife. She was nineteen; he was twenty-one.

Hindley was immediately smitten. Most of the men she knew she considered immature, but Brady dressed well and rode a motorbike. Everything about him fascinated her. 'Ian wore a black shirt today and looked smashing ... I love him,' she confided to her diary.

IAN BRADY

Although Ian Brady appeared to be a run-of-the-mill stock clerk, his mind was seething with sadistic fantasies. He had a collection of Nazi memorabilia and recordings of Nazi rallies. In his lunch hour, he read *Mein Kampf* and studied German grammar. A lifelong believer in the rightness of the Nazi cause, his only regret was that he could not join in its sadistic excesses.

Hindley described how the strength of her love for Brady had been part of the reason she allowed herself to be pushed into murder. She said he had 'such a powerful personality, such an overwhelming charisma. If he'd told me the moon was made of green cheese or that the sun rose in the west I would have believed him.'

For nearly a year Brady took no notice of her. 'The pig. He didn't even look at me today,' she wrote more than once.

Finally, in December 1961, he asked her out. 'Eureka!' her diary said. 'Today we have our first date. We are going to the cinema.' In varying accounts given by Hindley, she said that the film was *Judgment at Nuremberg* or *King of Kings*.

Soon Hindley had surrendered her virginity to Brady. She was madly in love with him and was writing schoolgirlishly: 'I hope Ian and I love each other all our lives and get married and are happy ever after.'

But their relationship was far more complex than that. Hindley was Brady's love slave. He talked to her of sexual perversions and lent her books on Nazi atrocities. They took pornographic photographs of each other and kept them in a scrapbook. Some showed the weals of a whip across her buttocks.

Hindley gave up baby-sitting and going to church. Within six months, Brady moved with Hindley into her grandmother's house. She was a frail woman who spent most of her time in bed, giving them the run of the place. Brady persuaded Hindley to bleach her hair a Teutonic blonde and dressed her in leather skirts and high-heeled boots. He called her Myra Hess – or Hessie – the name of a famous pianist who shared her surname with Hitler's deputy.

Hindley became hard and cruel, doing anything Brady asked. She did not even balk at procuring children for him to abuse, torture and kill. The first victim was sixteen-year-old Pauline Reade who disappeared on her way to a dance on 12 July 1963. Somehow they managed to persuade her to walk up to nearby Saddleworth Moor, where they killed and buried her in a shallow grave.

Four months later, Hindley hired a car and abducted twelve-year-old John Kilbride. When she returned the car, it was covered in peaty mud from the moors. Brady and Hindley laughed when they read about the massive police operation to find the missing boy.

In May 1964, Hindley bought a car of her own, a white Mini van. The following month, twelve-year-old Keith Bennett went missing. He too was buried on Saddleworth Moor. At Brady's behest, Hindley joined a local gun club and bought pistols for them both. They would go up to the moors for practice. While they were there, they would visit the graves of their victims. They would photograph each other kneeling on them.

On 26 December 1964, they abducted ten-year-old Lesley Ann Downey. This time they were determined to wring the maximum perverted pleasure out of their defenceless victim. They forced her to pose nude for pornographic photographs. Then they tortured her, recording her screams, before strangling her and burying her with the others on Saddleworth Moor.

Even this did not satisfy the depraved Brady. He wanted to extend his evil empire. He aimed to recruit Myra's sixteen-year-old brother-in-law, David Smith. Brady began trying to systematically corrupt Smith. He showed the youth his guns and talked to him about robbing a bank. He lent him books about the Marquis de Sade and got him to copy out quotations. 'Murder is a hobby and a supreme pleasure' and 'People are like maggots, small, blind, worthless fish-bait' Smith wrote in an exercise book under the guidance of Brady.

Brady believed they could lure anyone into their world of brutality and murder. He bragged to Smith about the murders he had already committed, saying he had photographs to prove it. They were drinking at the time and Smith thought he was joking, but Brady was determined to prove his claims.

Hindley and Brady decided to ensnare Smith into their vicious world by making him a party to murder. On 6 October 1965 Brady and Hindley picked up seventeen-year-old homosexual Edward Evans in a pub in Manchester. Smith had been invited to come around midnight. When he arrived, he heard a cry. 'Help him, Dave,' Hindley said. Smith rushed through into the sitting room to find a youth in a chair with Brady astride him. Brady had an axe in his hands and smashed it down on the boy's head. He hit him again and again – at least fourteen times.

'It's the messiest,' Brady said with some satisfaction. 'Usually it takes only one blow.'

He handed the axe to the dumbstruck Smith. This was a simple attempt to incriminate Smith by getting him to put his fingerprints on the murder weapon. Although Smith was terrified by what he had seen, he helped clean up the blood, while Brady and Hindley wrapped the body in a plastic sheet. The couple made jokes about the murder as they carried the corpse downstairs.

Hindley made a pot of tea and they all sat down.

'You should have seen the look on his face,' said Hindley, flushed with excitement, and she started reminiscing about the previous murders.

Smith could not believe all this was happening, but he realized that if he showed any sign of disgust or outrage he would be their next victim. After a decent interval, he made his excuses and left. When he got back to his flat, he was violently sick.

He told his wife what had happened and she urged him to go to the police. Armed with a knife and a screwdriver, they went out to a phone box at dawn and reported the murder. A police car picked the couple up and Smith told his lurid story to unbelieving policemen. Then at 8.40 a.m., the police dropped round to Hindley's house to check it out. To their horror, they found Edward Evans's body in the back bedroom.

Brady admitted killing Evans during an argument and tried to implicate Smith. Hindley only said: 'My story is the same at Ian's . . . Whatever he did, I did.' The only time she showed any emotion was when, while in custody, she was told that her dog had died. 'You fucking murderers,' she screamed at the police.

The police found a detailed plan that Brady had drawn up for the removal from the house of all clues to Evans's murder. One of the items mentioned was, curiously, Hindley's prayer book. When the police examined the prayer book, they found a left luggage ticket from Manchester station stuck down the spine. At the left luggage office, they found two suitcases which contained books on sexual perversion, coshes and pictures of Lesley Ann Downey naked and gagged. There was also the tape of her screams, which was later played to the stunned courtroom at Chester Assizes in April 1966. Other photographs showed Hindley posing beside graves on Saddleworth Moor. These helped the police locate the bodies of Lesley Ann Downey and John Kilbride.

As capital punishment had been ended in Britain the previous year, they were sentenced to life imprisonment. Brady did not bother to appeal. Hindley did so on the grounds that she should have been tried separately from Brady, but her appeal was rejected. They were also refused permission to see each other, though they were allowed to write.

Brady showed no contrition in prison and continued to see himself as a martyr in his own perverted cause. After nineteen years in solitary confinement in Durham prison, he was diagnosed as a psychopath and moved to Ashworth Psychiatric Hospital in Sefton where he died in 2017.

PRIME MOVER?

Hindley ceased writing to Brady in 1971 and petitioned to be released. When that was refused, a warder, who was Hindley's lesbian lover, organized an escape attempt. It failed and Hindley was sentenced to an additional year in jail.

She took an Open University degree and gave additional information on the whereabouts of the victims' graves in a bid for mercy. But Brady countered her every move by revealing more of her involvement in the crimes. He saw any attempt on her part to go free as disloyalty.

'The weight of our crimes justifies permanent imprisonment,' Brady told the Parole Board in 1982. 'I will not wish to be free in 1985 or even 2005.'

Myra Hindley died in prison in 2002, after hinting that there may have been one more victim, a young hitchhiker. Brady never addressed the matter or showed any remorse. Although he remained cold and ruthless, many suspect that Hindley was the prime mover in their sadistic campaign.

MARY BELL

The Tyneside Strangler *England, 1968*

When the strangled and mutilated three-year-old Brian Howe and four-year-old Martin Brown were found on a vacant lot in Newcastle, eleven-year-old Mary Bell said she had nothing to do with it. Confronted by the police, she tried to blame her friend Norma Bell (no relation). When the case went to trial Norma was acquitted of all charges, while Mary was convicted on two counts of manslaughter on the grounds of diminished responsibility.

At school, Mary was disruptive and expressed a desire to hurt people. She also had a reputation as an habitual liar. On 11 May 1968, Mary and Norma Bell were playing with a three-year-old boy on top of an old air-raid shelter when the boy fell and was seriously injured. The next day, the mothers of three children, all about six, complained to the police that Mary had choked them. A constable visited and gave Mary a reprimand, though no charges were filed.

Two weeks later, on the day before Mary's eleventh birthday, two boys playing in an abandoned house found the body of Martin Brown. Mary and Norma had followed the boys into the house and had to be ordered out when the police arrived. As no cause of death was immediately apparent, it was assumed that the four-year-old had swallowed pills from a discarded bottle found nearby.

Soon after, Norma's father found Mary choking his daughter and had to give her a slap to make her release her grip. Later a local nursery school was broken into and vandalized. Investigating, police found a note full of misspelling and obscenities, which included the line: 'We did murder Martin Brown.'

A few days later, Mary turned up at the Brown residence. When his grieving mother told her he was dead, Mary said: 'I know. I wanted to see him in his coffin.'

The following day, there was another break-in at the nursery school. This time the police were alerted by a newly installed alarm. Inside, they found Mary and Norma who denied that they were involved in the previous break-in. After they were released into the custody of their parents, Mary began spreading rumours that Norma had been responsible for the death of Martin Brown.

On 31 July, Brian Howe went missing. During the ensuing search, Mary told Brian's older sister that she had seen her brother playing on some concrete blocks on a vacant lot. His body was found there. He had been strangled and his legs, stomach and genitals had been mutilated with a pair of scissors found at the scene.

A pathologist suggested that the killer could have been a child since little force had been used. All the children in the area were questioned. Mary said that she had seen Brian being beaten by an eight-year-old carrying a pair of broken scissors. She immediately came under suspicion as the discovery of the scissors had not been made public. Norma said that she had been with Mary when they stumbled across Brian's body and Mary admitted killing him.

At the police station, Norma admitted that she had been with Mary when she attacked the boy, but had run away when she had 'gone all funny' and began strangling him. She had returned to find Mary cutting his hair and legs, and mutilating his penis with the scissors. A razor blade had also been used to carve the letter 'N', later amended to 'M' on the child's stomach. Norma told the police that the razor blade could be found under a rock, where they recovered it.

Confronted with this, Mary demanded to see a solicitor and accused the police of brainwashing her. She then retaliated by accusing Norma of the murder of Brian Howe. It was clear that the two girls were also involved in the death of Martin Brown.

MARY'S BACKGROUND

Mary Bell's mother Betty McCrickett rejected her when she was born on 26 May 1957, saying 'take the thing away from me'. Her care was taken over by her grandmother. However, Betty and later her husband Billy Bell continued to live in the family home in Gateshead. When Betty was pregnant with her second child, Mary, then just one, nearly died under the wheels of a lorry in what would be the first of a series of puzzling accidents. To add to her distress Betty and Billy threw Mary's grandmother out.

Betty said she could not cope with looking after two children and was often away. Mary was farmed out to relatives and friends, but Betty would not let her sister and her husband adopt the child. They noted that Mary never cried when she was hurt, but would scream and stamp when she did not get her own way. Though she was not spanked at home, she occasionally got a slap on the backside to halt a temper tantrum. Once she threatened to bash her uncle's face in and hit him with a toy gun.

The family feared for Mary's life. Another uncle hurt his back, saving Mary from falling from a window while she was in Betty's care. On another occasion, Mary was rushed to hospital to have her stomach pumped, having taken sleeping pills allegedly given to her by her mother. Five weeks later, a child who was out on the street with Mary was run over by a bus.

While Billy became a petty criminal, later arrested for armed robbery, Betty turned to prostitution and used Mary in the business. From an early age, Mary said, she was forced into sexual acts with men. Despite her hating this, she soon began taking money on her own account, while her mother became increasingly violent.

At Newcastle Assizes in December 1968, Norma Bell was freed while the trial judge Justice Cusack said of Mary: 'She has told four stories and, having told four stories, it is inconceivable that the jury would believe any one of them. She has fabricated. She is a very sick child. One can only hope that she can be given treatment to help her.'

Mary Bell was detained at Her Majesty's pleasure on the grounds that she was a grave risk to other children. Released in 1980, she was given a new identity and has gone on to become a mother and a grandmother.

Eighteen years after her release, Mary Bell co-operated with distinguished journalist Gitta Sereny, who had already published *The Case of Mary Bell* in 1972, to write *Cries Unheard: the Story of Mary Bell*. In it she revealed the grisly story of her early childhood, but not to assuage her guilt; she said: 'There are many unhappy, very disturbed kids out there who don't end up robbing families of their children.'

PHOOLAN DEVI

The Bandit Queen *India, 1981–83*

Dubbed a 'modern-day Indian Robin Hood and Bonnie Parker, with a touch of Gloria Steinem' by the *Washington Post*, Phoolan Devi killed more than twenty high-caste men in revenge for the murder of her lover and her own gang rape. After eleven years in jail, she went on to become a member of parliament, despite not being able to read or write, and a Bollywood film was made about her.

Born in 1963 to the lowly Mallah, boatman or peasant caste, Phoolan Devi was not content with her lot. At the age of eleven, she protested that her family's meagre plot of land was taken by a male cousin because her father only had daughters. She called him a thief and taunted him until he knocked her unconscious with a brick.

Her parents then married their troublesome daughter off to a man three times her age in exchange for a cow. This was common practice in rural India. She conceded that her parents did this with the best of intentions. He had money and they thought she would have a better life.

'No one knew that he was not a man, he was a monster,' she said.

Just eleven, she was terrified of sex and wailed every time he forced himself on her. He took a second wife. The two of them beat her and treated her like a slave. At twelve, she ran away, but her parents sent her back. Eventually her husband abandoned her. In Indian society this was a disgrace and her mother advised her to commit suicide. Instead she married a cousin, who already had a wife. Scorned by the men of the land-owning Thakur caste, she was said to bathe naked in the sacred Yamuna river – a sacrilege.

Meanwhile she continued her battle with her cousin, arguing the case before the Allahabad High Court. In retaliation her cousin accused her of stealing from his house. She was jailed, beaten and raped by the police.

It is not quite clear what happened next. Whether she escaped or was kidnapped, she ended up in the hands of a bandit leader named Babu Gujar, who brutalized her for three days. Babu Gujar was upper-caste, but his deputy Vikram Mallah was a member of her caste. He shot Babu Gujar dead and took Phoolan as his mistress. Together they robbed and looted, held up trains, ransacked upper-caste villages and homes, murdered and kidnapped. They hid out in bandit country – the ravines and jungles of Uttar and Madhya Pradesh – and worshipped in the temple of Durga, the weapon-wielding Hindu goddess depicted riding a tiger.

But Vikram Mallah was killed by the Ram brothers, two upper-caste bandits, in revenge for the murder of Babu Gujar. The Ram brothers then took Phoolan to the village of Behmai where she was imprisoned and repeatedly raped. In a further humiliation, she was forced to walk the length of the village naked to collect water while the Thakur men looked on, hooting and jeering.

Eventually, Phoolan was rescued and went on to form her own gang. They returned to Behmai in police uniforms. Phoolan carried a Sten gun and wore a bandolier of ammunition across her chest. She demanded that the Thakur hand over the Ram brothers. Her men searched the village, looting as they went. When the Ram brothers were not found, the Thakur men were lined up and shot. Twenty-two fell dead. Phoolan later claimed that she had not pulled the trigger herself, but it was clear that she had instigated the massacre.

The killings made Phoolan a folk hero among lower-caste

Indians, who called her the Bandit Queen. A massive police man-hunt was underway, but after two years they had failed to capture her. In 1983, the government of Indira Gandhi decided to nego-tiate. By this time Phoolan was ill and many of her men had been killed. She agreed to surrender, but only in Madhya Pradesh, not in Uttar Pradesh where she feared she would be killed. Her conditions for surrender were that she lay down her arms before a picture of Mahatma Gandhi and the goddess Durga, not the police; that she would not be subjected to the death penalty and that none of her gang members would serve for more than eight years in jail; that her beloved younger brother be given a govern-ment job and her father a plot of land, and that her entire family, including the family cow and goat, be escorted to the surrender ceremony by the police.

A crowd of ten thousand turned out for the surrender, where Phoolan handed over her gun and twenty-five bullets to the chief minister of Madhya Pradesh. She was charged with forty-eight criminal offences, including the murders in Behmai. Her trial was postponed repeatedly for eleven years, while Madhya Pradesh and Uttar Pradesh argued over jurisdiction. Eventually a new low-caste government was elected in Uttar Pradesh. The charges against her were dropped and she was released in 1994.

Two years later she was elected MP for the constituency of Mirzapur in Uttar Pradesh as a champion of the poor and oppressed. She lost her seat in 1998, but was re-elected the fol-lowing year.

In 2001, she was shot by three masked men outside her bun-galow in Delhi. With three bullets in her head and two in her body, she was declared dead when she arrived at hospital. The chief suspect, Sher Singh Rana, surrendered to the police. His motivation was thought to be revenge for the Behmai massacre. He was sentenced to life imprisonment.

Bandit Queen

The movie *Bandit Queen* was based on the book *India's Bandit Queen: The True Story of Phoolan Devi* by the Indian author Mala Sen. It premiered at the Cannes Film Festival in 1994. Phoolan fiercely disputed the accuracy of the film and fought to get it banned, even threatening to immolate herself outside a theatre if it was not withdrawn. She also filed a lawsuit to keep it out of the cinema on the grounds that it was an unauthorized invasion of her privacy.

'They are raping me all over again and selling me on the screen,' she said. 'They are selling my honour.'

Eventually she accepted a monetary settlement from the producers and the film brought her international recognition. The film also caused problems for the India censor because of its violent rape scenes, nudity and depiction of sensitive political issues. Nevertheless, it won several accolades at the National Film Awards in India, including Best Feature Film in Hindi.

DOROTHEA PUENTE

The Death House Landlady *America, 1982–88*

Although she looked like a kindly grandmother, Dorothea Puente was a ruthless killer. She ran a boarding house for the elderly and infirm. When she tired of tenants, she would kill them and bury them in the backyard, while continuing to cash their social security cheques. In her second-storey apartment, the police found silk dresses, $110 bottles of Giorgio perfume and a well-stocked liquor cabinet – alcohol was something her tenants were denied. Victims' pensions even funded a facelift.

I n November 1988, Detective John Cabrera visited the boarding house at 1426 F Street in Sacramento, California. He was looking for fifty-one-year-old Alvaro 'Bert' Montoya, a schizophrenic with learning difficulties who had been a tenant there. His social worker had reported him missing.

The owner, Mrs Dorothea Puente, rented out rooms to social services cases. The house was known to give off a putrid odour that she blamed variously on a backed-up sewer, dead rats rotting or the fish emulsion she used as a fertilizer. To hide the smell she dumped gallons of bleach and bags of lime in the back garden.

Cabrera knocked on the front door and asked Puente whether he could look around. In the backyard, he discovered that the soil had recently been disturbed. A police team were called in and began digging. They quickly came across what Cabrera said looked like 'shreds of cloth and beef jerky'. Progress was then hindered by what seemed to be the root of a tree. Cabrera climbed down and pulled on it. When it came away, he discovered he was holding a bone. Next, they found a shoe with a foot still inside it. When Puente was told that the police had found human remains, she appeared shocked.

The next morning, a mechanical digger unearthed the rest of a skeleton that belonged to a small white-haired female. Then a second body was found. As workmen took a drill to a concrete slab, Mrs Puente appeared and asked Cabrera whether she was under arrest. When he said no, she asked if she could go and have a cup of coffee in the nearby Clarion Hotel.

Three more bodies were found under the concrete slab, another under the gazebo. Four hours had passed before anyone noticed that Mrs Puente had not returned. In all seven bodies were found. Alvaro Montoya's was found under a newly planted apricot tree.

Police searched the boarding house and discovered that Puente had been fraudulently cashing the victims' benefit cheques. She was also making a good income from her living tenants who were paying $350 a month for board and lodgings. Boarders told the police that others went missing after Puente said they were unwell and she was 'taking them upstairs to make them feel better'.

After Puente had drunk her coffee, she took a bus to Los Angeles. There she met fifty-nine-year-old retired carpenter Charles Willgues in a downtown bar. Once she had established that he was receiving $576 a month from social security, she suggested they move in together. Willgues declined but took her for a chicken dinner. Back in his apartment, he switched on the TV to see his dinner companion, along with footage of bodies being disinterred. He called the TV station, who contacted the police.

Puente was arrested in her motel and flown back to Sacramento. She denied killing anyone, but admitted cashing their benefit cheques. Charged with nine counts of murder, she pleaded not guilty at the Sacramento Municipal Court on 31 March 1989.

Her trial began in February 1993. The prosecutor John O'Mara said that Puente murdered her lodgers to steal their government cheques. She had selected victims who had no relatives and no friends who would ask questions. Sleeping pills were used to knock them out. She then suffocated them and hired convicts to dig the holes in her garden to bury them.

While there were no eyewitnesses, toxicological tests revealed that the remains contained traces of Dalmane (flurazepam), a prescription-strength sleeping pill. The trial dragged on for a year and the jury were out for a month, before finding Puente guilty on three counts of murder. But they were deadlocked on whether she should suffer the death penalty. In the end, she was spared. One juror said: 'Executing Puente would be like executing your grandma.'

Puente was given two life sentences without the possibility of parole along with a concurrent fifteen-year-to-life sentence. She died of natural causes in prison in Chowchilla, California, on 27 March 2011 at the age of eighty-two, still protesting her innocence.

A life of crime

Although she appeared to be a harmless old lady, Puente had been a lifelong criminal. At sixteen, she moved to Olympia, Washington, where she called herself 'Sheri' and augmented her income turning tricks in a motel. In the autumn of 1945, she met twenty-two-year-old Fred McFaul and had two daughters. One was raised by his mother, the other adopted. When the marriage broke up, she returned to prostitution, supplementing her earnings with petty crime. She was convicted of forgery, served four years in jail, then skipped town while she was on probation. Pregnant by a man she barely knew, she gave that child up for adoption too.

In 1952, she married her second husband, Axel Johansson, a merchant seaman. While he was away at sea, she worked as a prostitute. In 1960, she was convicted of residing in a brothel in Sacramento and vagrancy.

Released, she got work as a nurse's aide, looking after elderly and disabled people in private homes. In 1968, she opened a halfway house for alcoholics. The halfway house was closed after running up $10,000 in debt.

She then took over a boarding house at 2100 F Street in Sacramento and, in 1976, she married one of the tenants. Her new husband was fifty-two-year-old Pedro Angel Montalvo, a violent alcoholic. The marriage lasted only a few months and she retained the name from a previous marriage, Puente.

In 1978, she was convicted of forging cheques she had stolen from her tenants. Three years later, she began renting an upstairs apartment in 1426 F Street. Sixty-one-year-old Ruth Munroe moved in as her business partner, bringing with her $6,000 in cash. Soon after Munroe began to feel ill and died of an overdose of codeine and Tylenol.

A month later, Puente was arrested and charged with drugging four elderly people and stealing their valuables. She was sentenced to five years. Released after three, she was ordered not to handle government cheques issued to others and to stay away from the elderly.

When Puente left jail, seventy-seven-year-old Everson Gillmouth was waiting at the gates in a 1980 red Ford pickup. They moved back into the apartment at 1426 F Street. Gillmouth's body was found dumped on the banks of the Sacramento River in a make-shift coffin constructed by handyman Ismael Florez, then owner of the red Ford pickup. The remains would lie unidentified for three years in the city morgue while Puente went on collecting his pension.

When the owner of 1426 F Street moved out, Puente took over. She arranged to take in homeless clients. Puente was thought useful by local social workers because she accepted the hardest clients to place – drug addicts and alcoholics, and people who were violent or verbally abusive. Federal parole agents visited Puente fifteen times in the two years leading up to the discovery in the backyard and never realized she was running a boarding house for the elderly – a direct violation of her parole.

MARIA GRUBER, IRENE LEIDOLF, STEPHANIJA MAYER & WALTRAUD WAGNER

Lainz Angels of Death *Austria, 1983–89*

In Lainz General Hospital in Vienna, four nurse's aides working night shifts murdered possibly hundreds of elderly and infirm patients who annoyed them. Waltraud Wagner, the leader, would remark that these victims had received 'a ticket to God' or had booked 'a meeting with the undertaker'. News of the killings stunned Austria. The trial of Vienna's 'death angels' would become the biggest murder trial in Austria since the Second World War.

I n 1982, twenty-three-year-old Waltraud Wagner began work as a nurse's aide at Lainz General Hospital's Pavilion Five, which housed elderly patients, many of whom were terminally ill. In the spring of 1983, a seventy-year-old patient asked her to put her out of her misery. Wagner did so with an overdose of morphine. She went on to use insulin and tranquillizers to despatch troublesome patients who wet the bed or demanded attention at inconvenient times.

Over the years, Wagner was joined on the graveyard shift in Pavilion Five by Maria Gruber, a single mother and nursing-school dropout, and Irene Leidolf, who had a husband at home but preferred hanging out with the other women. Both these accomplices were in their twenties and, like Wagner, came from large families in rural Austria with little higher education.

The murderous team was completed by Stephanija Mayer, a divorced grandmother who had emigrated from Yugoslavia in 1987. She was twenty years older that Wagner, but her maturity proved no constraint.

Wagner taught them how to administer lethal injections to anyone they found annoying. These included patients who made a complaint, summoned the nurse during the night, snored loudly, soiled the sheets or refused their medication. Any one of these infractions would be a death sentence.

More sadistically, they would give what Wagner called 'the water cure'. The patient's head would be tipped back, their tongued depressed and their nostrils pinched. Then water would be poured down their throat. It was a slow and agonizing death, though virtually undetectable, as elderly patients frequently had fluid in their lungs when they died.

The murder rate seems to have accelerated in 1987. By 1988 rumours were rife, but the head of the ward, Dr Franz Xavier Pesendorfer, made no timely effort to investigate. The Angels of Death were eventually betrayed by their own hubris. Often enjoying a drink after work, they were finally caught out in February 1989 when a doctor seated nearby overheard them laughing about the death of elderly patient Julia Drapal. She had been given the water cure for refusing her medication and calling Wagner a slut. He reported the matter to the police who, after a six-week investigation, made their arrests.

Between them, the four women admitted killing forty-nine patients who were bothersome or too demanding. But later they retracted substantial parts of their confessions, claiming that they had killed only a handful of patients, who were terminally ill, to alleviate their pain.

After a number of bodies were exhumed, they were charged with the forty-two counts of murder. The state prosecutor Ernst Kloyber said that the number of victims was much higher and would probably never be known. Some estimates put the number as high as three hundred. In court, he evoked the medical experiments in the Nazi death camps. 'This was no mercy killing,' he told the jury at the trial in 1991, 'but cold-blooded murder of helpless people, which reminds us of a period in Austrian history none of us likes to remember.'

The judge dismissed Wagner's claim that they were alleviating pain, pointing to her use of the 'water cure'.

'These patients were gasping for breath for up to half-a-day before they died,' he said. 'You cannot call that pain relief.'

Wagner was convicted of fifteen counts of murder, seventeen counts of attempted murder and two counts of causing deliberate bodily harm. She was sentenced to life. Leidolf was also sentenced to life. Both immediately appealed. Mayer was sentenced to twenty years, Gruber to fifteen for manslaughter and attempted murder.

Commentators pointed out that the case spoke volumes about a society that was increasingly obsessed with youth and material well-being and insensitive to age and infirmity. A survey showed that twenty-five per cent of those questioned thought that euthanasia was justifiable in some circumstances.

A front page editorial in the Viennese newspaper *Die Presse* said: 'The most recent investigation into what is "holy" to the Austrians showed it quite clearly: Their own health is most important to the individual, but the general protection of human life – in the narrow, as well as the broadest sense – ranked behind protecting material goods. To damage an auto appears to be much worse than visiting injustice or harm on one's fellow man.'

But the state prosecutor stood firm in the face of public opinion. He said: 'It's a small step from killing the terminally ill to the killing of insolent, burdensome patients, and from there to that which was known under the Third Reich as euthanasia. It is a door that must never be opened again.'

Public outrage

Dr Pesendorfer was suspended in April 1989 because he failed to pursue rumours of mass killings in his department that had been circulating for at least a year. He defended his actions, saying he had alerted the authorities, doctors and supervisory nurses and ordered autopsies as soon as suspicions were raised.

'What more could I have done?' he said. 'The dead were not victims of the system but victims of crimes that could not have been anticipated and prevented.'

After the nurses' confessions, the health service was angrily criticized. Hildegard Fach, the head of the national union of nurses and nurse's aides, said that regulations were routinely violated in Austrian hospitals as nurse's aides are allowed to give injections. Their duties are supposed to be limited to cleaning, feeding and assisting patients.

Nurses were also abused by the public. One said she had been spat on.

There was further outrage in 2008 when Wagner and Leidolf were released early for good behaviour. Gruber and Mayer, convicted on lesser charges, had been released earlier and given new identities.

The Austrian newspaper *Heute* carried the headline: 'The death angels are getting out.'

'It's inhumane and immoral to execute a killer,' one Viennese citizen was quoted as saying, 'but it's not fair to their victims' loved ones when a killer can look forward to a nice life outside prison.'

AILEEN WUORNOS

The Florida Highway Killer *America, 1989–90*

An habitual criminal, Aileen Wuornos developed an obsessive hatred of men and fed it by killing like a man. For a year, she ranged throughout Florida leaving a wake of terror behind. Her story was told in the movie *Monster*, starring Charlize Theron.

I n May 1974, at the age of eighteen, Aileen Wournos – using the alias 'Sandra Kretsch' – was jailed in Colorado for disorderly conduct, drunk driving and firing a .22 pistol from a moving vehicle. She left town before her trial and returned to her origins in Michigan, where she was arrested for assault and disturbing the peace when she hurled a pool ball at a bartender. For this, and outstanding charges of driving without a licence and drinking while driving, she was fined $105. When her brother Keith suddenly died, Aileen was surprised to receive an insurance payout of $10,000 – but quickly squandered the money.

Back on the road, Aileen set off for Florida. On 20 May 1981, she was arrested in Edgeworth for armed robbery of a convenience store, being released from prison in June 1983. Over the next two years she faced numerous charges: passing forged cheques, car theft and a number of driving offences. On many occasions police found a firearm in her car.

In June 1986 Aileen met up with thirty-three-year-old Tyria Moore in a gay bar in Daytona, Florida. They were lovers for a year or so, but remained close companions for four years and were regularly in trouble as they drifted round Florida, living in trailer parks and seedy apartments. Most of the time, Aileen adopted the alias of 'Susan Blahovec'. She worked truck stops and bars, or thumbed lifts, in pursuit of her chosen trade of prostitution, but she was becoming increasingly belligerent and always carried a loaded pistol in her purse.

On 30 November 1989, a car belonging to fifty-one-year-old Richard Mallory was found abandoned, his wallet and its contents scattered close by. On 13 December, his body, fully dressed, was found in woods north-west of Daytona Beach; he had been shot three times with a .22 pistol. On 1 June 1990, the naked corpse of forty-three-year-old David Spears, who had been missing since 19 May, was found in woodland forty miles north of Tampa. He had been shot six times with a .22-calibre weapon.

Charles Carskaddon, aged forty, vanished on 31 May, somewhere on the road from Bonneville, Missouri. His naked body was found north of Tampa on 6 June. He had been shot nine times with a .22 pistol and his car was discovered the following day, with his lethal .45 automatic and personal belongings stolen. Yet the police still refused to acknowledge that a serial killer was at work in Florida.

Sixty-five-year-old Peter Siems was last seen when he left home near Palm Beach on 7 June, bound for Arkansas to visit relatives. On 4 July, his car was found, wrecked and abandoned, two hundred miles to the north. Witnesses to the crash were able to describe two women leaving the vehicle, one blonde and one brunette. The blonde was bleeding from an injury, and a bloody palm print was obtained from the car trunk. As Siems was considerably older than the previous victims, and had become a missionary, it seemed unlikely that he had accepted an offer of sex – most likely that he had picked up two apparently harmless hitch-hikers.

Eugene Burress, aged fifty, was reported missing from Ocala, in central Florida, on 30 July. His fully dressed body was discovered in Ocala National Forest, shot twice with a .22 pistol, on 4 August. Scattered around were his credit cards and a cash bag from a local bank – empty.

Also missing from Ocala, on 11 September, was Dick Humphreys, a fifty-six-year-old retired police chief from Alabama. The following day, his clothed body was found, shot seven times with a .22-calibre weapon. His car was found two weeks later, some hundred miles to the north, but was not traced to Humphreys until 13 October, when his badge and other personal items were discovered seventy miles to the south-east.

The corpse of sixty-year-old Walter Antonio, a trucker and reserve police officer from Marritt Island, on Florida's east coast, was discovered near the north-west coast on 19 November. He was naked apart from his socks, his clothes later being found in a neighbouring county and his car back east on 24 November. He had been shot three times in the back and once in the head, and his police badge, nightstick, handcuffs and flashlight had been stolen.

Intense media pressure at last forced the police to recognize that this was a series of related killings. Over the next three weeks, searches of motel receipts uncovered the movements of 'Lee Blahovec', 'Lori Grody' and 'Cammie Greene', and fingerprint analysis identified the wanted woman as Aileen Wuornos. Meanwhile, Aileen was raising money by pawning identifiable property stolen from her victims – and leaving more telltale fingerprints.

On 9 January 1991, the police finally caught up with Aileen in a Florida biker bar. Tyria Moore was traced to her sister's home in Pennsylvania and agreed to assist the police in developing their murder case. Then, in jail on 16 January, Aileen confessed to six killings, insisting that they had all been in self-defence, and denied the murder of Peter Siems.

Aileen Wuornos stood trial on 13 January 1992, charged with the murder of Richard Mallory. As the only witness for her defence, she testified to a violent rape and beating by him, only shooting him when he threatened to kill her. There was no evidence presented of Mallory's character, and on 27 January the jury found Aileen guilty, recommending the death penalty two days later. She shouted out: 'I'm innocent! I was raped! I hope you get raped! Scumbags of America!'

Ten months later – and far too late – a TV reporter unearthed the fact that Mallory had indeed served ten years in another state for violent rape.

In April, Aileen pleaded guilty to the killing of Spears, Burress and Humphreys, and received the death sentence for all three. She also offered to show where the body of Peter Siems was hidden, but nothing was found and the police theorized that this was merely a ruse to obtain a few days away from prison.

Aileen Wuornos, consistently proclaiming her innocence and lodging appeals, remained on Death Row in Florida for ten years, finally going to the electric chair on 9 October 2002.

Early days of a monster

Aileen Carol Wuornos was born in Rochester, Michigan, on 29 February 1956, the second child of teenage parents Diane Wuornos and Leo Pitman, who separated before she was born. Her father was later sentenced to life imprisonment for raping a child and hanged himself in his prison cell. Her young mother, unable to stand her 'crying, unhappy babies', gave Aileen and her elder brother Keith into the care and adoption of her parents.

At age six, 'Lee' – as she liked to call herself – suffered scarring to her face when she and Keith were setting fires with lighter fluid. She became pregnant before the age of fifteen and her son was born in a Detroit maternity hospital on 23 March 1971, and was given up for adoption. When her grandmother died some months later, Aileen dropped out of school and took to the roads as a wandering prostitute, hitch-hiking from state to state.

Aileen's victims

30 November 1989	Richard Mallory, 51; shot, body found 13 December
19–20 May 1990	David Spears, 43; shot, body found 1 June
31 May 1990	Charles Carskaddon, 40; shot, body found 6 June
7 June 1990	Peter Siems, 65; body undiscovered
30 July 1990	Eugene Burress, 50; shot, body found 4 August
11 September 1990	Dick Humphreys, 56; shot body found next day
Oct–Nov 1990	Walter Antonio, 60; shot, body found 19 November

BEVERLEY ALLITT

England's Angel of Death *England, 1991*

Alone on the night shift in the children's ward at Grantham and Kesteven Hospital in Lincolnshire, Beverley Allitt administered lethal injections of insulin and potassium, and attempted suffocation, on twenty-three children in her charge, killing four and leaving a further nine irreparably damaged – all in fifty-nine days.

O n 23 February 1991, just two days after Allitt had started on Children's Ward Four, seven-year-old Liam Taylor was brought in with a chest infection. Allitt assured his parents he would be okay – she would take good care of him. But two hours later when they returned, they found that he had collapsed and had to be revived.

The couple were relieved and grateful when Allitt volunteered for an extra night shift to look after him. After other staff had been out of sight, Allitt called for a crash team. Although none of the alarms he had been hooked up to had gone off, he had suffered a cardiac arrest. Despairing doctors soon concluded that he had suffered severe brain damage, leaving no reason to resuscitate him. Two hours later, his parents agreed to switch off the life support system and Liam was dead.

The doctors could not understand how he had died. Cardiac arrest is almost unheard of in a young child. A post-mortem revealed heart damage usually seen after a lifetime of heavy smoking or drinking.

Ten days later, eleven-year-old Timothy Hardwick was admitted to Ward Four. He had cerebral palsy and had suffered an epileptic fit. Again Allitt seemed to lavish care on the child. Suddenly, again when no one was looking, Timothy also suffered a cardiac arrest. Once more, the death was unexplained, but no one called the police.

In the same bed just five days later, fourteen-month-old Kayley Desmond suffered a cardiac arrest while being treated by Allitt. She was revived and rushed to the intensive care unit at the Queen's Medical Centre in Nottingham, amid concern that she might have suffered brain damage when starved of oxygen. It was assumed that this had occurred when, as a bad feeder, she had inhaled milk and stopped breathing. However, under her right armpit there was a needle puncture with a small bubble of air behind it as if someone had injected her ineptly.

Another ten days passed before five-month-old Paul Crampton was admitted to the ward with mild bronchitis. Responding well to treatment, he was due to be discharged four days later. But three times, his system collapsed with hypoglycaemia. After the third attack, he was rushed to the Queen's Medical Centre, with Allitt in the ambulance, where he was discovered to have high levels of insulin in his blood.

The following day, five-year-old Bradley Gibson was admitted, suffering from pneumonia. During the night, he complained of pain in the arm where his antibiotic drip was attached. He was attended by Allitt. On the second occasion, he suffered a cardiac arrest. For half-an-hour, the crash team battled to save him – successfully. He too was taken to Queen's.

The day after that, two-year-old Yik Hung 'Henry' Chan was admitted after a fall from a bedroom window had resulted in a fractured skull. Attended by Allitt, the child was crying. Summoned, other staff found him blue with his back arched. He was revived with oxygen. When this happened a second time, Henry, too, was rushed to Queen's.

Four days later, it was the turn of identical twins Becky and Katie Phillips, who were just two months old. Becky was admitted for observation after suffering from acute gastro-enteritis. She was untroubled for the first two days because Allitt had been off. When she returned, Allitt told another nurse that Becky looked hypoglycaemic. Nevertheless, she was taken home the next day and died in the night. No reason could be found, except for the unusually high level of insulin in her blood. Her demise was simply dismissed as a cot death.

As a precaution, Katie was sent to hospital for observation, and was also cared for by Allitt. The night after admission, she suffered a cardiac arrest. Emergency treatment saved her life, but the same thing happened again two days later. Rushed to Queen's she was found to have suffered brain damage. She had cerebral palsy, paralysis of the right side and damage to her eyesight and hearing. What's more, five of her ribs were broken. This was put down to frantic efforts to resuscitate her. But Katie's mother Sue was so grateful to Allitt for saving her daughter's life she asked her to be her godmother.

A few days later, six-year-old Michael Davidson was admitted after being accidentally shot with an airgun. Allitt helped prepare an intravenous antibiotic. When it was administered, the child's heart stopped beating. But he was resuscitated and, eventually, discharged.

That day two-month-old Chris Peasgood was admitted with breathing difficulties. While he was put in an oxygen tent, Allitt suggested that his parents go and have a cup of tea. When they returned they found a crash team in action. A nurse had discovered that the alarm indicating he had stopped breathing had been turned off and Allitt standing beside the bed doing nothing.

Nevertheless Allitt assured Chris's parents that he would be all right, but he suffered another cardiac arrest during the night. Fearing that he was dying, the child was christened before being rushed to Queen's where he recovered.

Christopher King was a month old when he was admitted for an operation. He became inexplicably ill before going to surgery and had to be revived with oxygen. The operation was a success, but he had to be revived four more times before he was sent to Queen's.

Seven-week-old Patrick Elston had been playing and laughing when his parents had dropped him off for a check-up. In Allitt's care, he had stopped breathing. He was rushed to Queen's, but not before he had suffered brain damage. After fifty-nine days, the doctors at Queen's were beginning to ask the question: Why were so many children coming into their care from Ward Four?

An asthmatic, fifteen-month-old Claire Peck had been admitted to the ward on 18 April, but had been discharged two days later. Then, after a coughing fit, she was brought back in on 22 April. The Pecks were ushered away while their daughter was being treated. Left alone, Allitt suddenly cried out: 'Arrest! Arrest!'

Doctors came running and revived the child, but as soon as she was left alone with Allitt the same thing happened again. This time the doctors could not save her. Claire's mother Susan, holding the dead child, noticed that everyone else was upset, but Allitt just stood there staring.

The authorities first suspected that legionaires' disease was at work. Although no virus was found, the ward was meticulously scrubbed. Then the drug lignocaine, used in cardiac arrest, was found in Claire's body. A powerful poison, it was clear evidence of murder.

The police were called in and it was discovered, by checking the rotas, that Allitt was the only person who was present every time there was a medical emergency. Notes covering Paul Crampton's stay were missing. Allitt was suspended, but the parents of the Phillips twins had so much faith in her, they hired a private detective to clear her name.

After her arrest, a missing ward diary was found in her home. She denied all charges and appeared in Nottingham Crown Court in February 1993. The prosecution showed that Allitt had the means and the opportunity to commit the crime – but what of the motive? Consultant paediatrician Professor Roy Meadow told the court that Allitt exhibited all the symptoms of Munchausen's Syndrome and Munchausen's Syndrome by Proxy. In the first condition, the sufferer seeks medical attention by self-harm or faking complaints – Allitt's extensive medical record confirmed this. Even while she had been out on bail, she had been admitted to hospital, complaining of an enlarged right breast. It was discovered that she had been injecting herself with water.

The second condition is usually exhibited by mothers, where they seek medical attention by complaining that their offspring is suffering fictitious complaints or inflicting actual abuse. Professor Meadow said that to suffer from both Munchausen's Syndrome and Munchausen's Syndrome by Proxy was extremely rare, but he came across around forty cases of the proxy condition a year.

Allitt was not present in court for much of the trial as she was suffering from anorexia nervosa. When she returned to the dock, the judge told her:

> You have been found guilty of the most terrible crimes. You killed, tried to kill or seriously harmed thirteen children, many of them tiny babies. They had been entrusted to your care. You have brought grief to their families. You have sown a seed of doubt in those who should have faith in the integrity of care their children receive in hospital. Hopefully, the grief felt by the families will become easier to bear, but it will always be there. You are seriously disturbed. You are cunning and manipulative and you have shown no remorse for the trail of destruction you have left behind you. I accept it is all the result of the severe personality disorder you have. But you are and remain a very serious danger to others.

He gave her thirteen concurrent terms of life imprisonment, serving a minimum of thirty years and only to be released then if she was considered no danger to the public. Remitted to

Rampton Secure Hospital, she admitted to some of the murders and attempted murders. Meanwhile the families and the victims who survived disabled will have to live a lifetime with what she has done.

BACKGROUND

Allitt showed disturbing symptoms of a mental disorder from an early age. One of four children, she sought attention by wearing dressings and casts over supposed wounds that she would allow no one to examine. Growing overweight as an adolescent, her attention-seeking became aggressive. She was also known to self-harm and hopped from doctor to doctor, seeking treatment for fictitious ailments. These included gall bladder pain, headaches, urinary infections, uncontrolled vomiting, blurred vision, minor injuries, back trouble, ulcers and appendicitis, resulting in the removal of a perfectly healthy appendix. The scar failed to heal as she kept picking at the wound.

While training as a nurse, she had a poor attendance record, frequently being absent with supposed illnesses. She was also suspected of odd behaviour, including smearing faeces on the walls of the nursing home. Her boyfriend accused her of being aggressive, manipulative and deceptive. She falsely claimed to be pregnant and told people he had AIDS. And she accused a friend of his of rape, though she did not go to the police. The relationship ended when Allitt took another student nurse as a lover.

KRISTEN GILBERT

America's Angel of Death *USA, 1990–96*

It was noted that on Ward C at the Veterans Affairs Medical Center in Northampton, Massachusetts, there were an unusual number of cardiac arrests among patients who had not suffered heart problems before. So many of them were under the care of Kristen Gilbert that her co-workers began to call her the 'Angel of Death'.

Kristen was a calm and competent nurse, who won the admiration of those that worked alongside her. But in 1990, after she returned from maternity leave, it was noted that the rate of cardiac arrests on Ward C tripled from what it had been over the previous three years.

After the birth of her second son in 1993, the Gilberts' marriage began to fall apart. She took a shine to James Perrault, a hospital police officer. Under Veterans Affairs rules, the hospital police had to be on hand during any medical emergency. They became lovers and it was even alleged that an AIDS patient suddenly died of a heart attack so that she could leave early on a date with him. Kristen Gilbert's husband Glenn then found his food tasted odd and was convinced that she was trying to kill him. Soon after Kristen moved in with Perrault.

The high mortality rate on Ward C put all the nurses under suspicion. It was then noted that stocks of the drug epinephrine – a synthetic form of adrenaline – were going missing. It was a heart stimulant that, if injected unnecessarily, could cause cardiac arrest. This gave Kristen an opportunity to show off her nursing skills and flirt with Perrault. Three fellow nurses reported their suspicions to the authorities.

While under investigation, Gilbert bought a device to disguise her voice and called the hospital saying that bombs had been planted there. Staff and patients, many of whom were sick and elderly, had to be evacuated. She was arrested and served fifteen months. While she was in prison, investigators began to exhume some of the bodies of those who had died on her shift. They were found to contain epinephrine, though they had no history of heart complaints.

In 1998, aged thirty, she was indicted for the murder of four men and the attempted murder of three others. However, the Assistant US Attorney said that thirty-seven men had died during her shifts between January 1995 and February 1996. In the seven years she had worked at the VA hospital, 350 had died on her shifts and she was thought to have been responsible for eighty of the deaths.

Perrault testified against her, saying that she had told him during a telephone conversation: 'I did it. You wanted to know, I killed all those guys by injection.'

The defence maintained that she had only said that after suffering psychiatric problems following the break-up of their stormy affair. There were no witnesses to Gilbert administering the drug, so all the evidence was circumstantial.

In 2001, Kristen Gilbert was found guilty of three counts of first-degree murder, one count of second-degree murder and two counts of attempted murder. While there was no death penalty in the state of Massachusetts, the crimes had taken place on Federal property, so she did face the prospect of, herself, facing a lethal injection. The defence argued that it would be punishment enough to lead a life 'where you can't walk out into a field, or see snow or play with a puppy'.

This won little sympathy among the relatives of the victims, but the jury decided against the death penalty because of the affect it might have on her two young sons. Gilbert was sentenced to four consecutive terms of life imprisonment without possibility of parole, plus twenty years. She dropped her appeal after the US Supreme Court ruled that she risked the death penalty again on retrial. Her life sentence would be served at the Carswell Federal Medical Center in Fort Worth, Texas.

Lizzie Borden

Born Kristen Heather Strickland in Fall River, Massachusetts, in 1967, she showed signs as a teenager of being a pathological liar. She made unfounded claims of being a distant relation of the infamous Lizzie Borden, who reputedly despatched her mother and father with forty whacks in Fall River in 1892, though she was acquitted.

Former boyfriends accused her of being strange and controlling, even resorting to verbal and physical abuse, or tampering with their cars. When all else failed, she would fake suicide attempts.

Graduating from high school a year and a half early, she went on to college. Working as a home-health aide, she once badly scalded a child with learning difficulties, though no action was taken against her. In 1988, she became a registered nurse and eloped with Glenn Gilbert. Their marriage was full of rows and, on one occasion, she chased him with a butcher's knife.

KATHERINE KNIGHT

Cannibal Casserole-Maker *Australia, 2000*

Australian slaughterhouse worker Katherine Knight had a history of violence, but when she awoke on the morning of 1 March 2000, she claimed she could not remember killing her common-law husband, skinning his corpse, cooking parts of his body and serving them up ready for his children to eat.

When police were called out to slaughterhouse worker Katherine Knight's house at 84 St Andrews Street in Aberdeen, New South Wales, by her husband John Price's boss who was suspicious that John had failed to turn up at work, they were met by a horrifying scene. Blood splatters and handprints covered the walls in the hallway and the police 'located the victim's exterior layers of skin hanging from a hook in a doorway arch into the lounge room. They then located the victim's decapitated remains on the lounge room floor near a small foyer leading to the front door.' Searching the rest of the house, they found Katherine Knight comatose and snoring loudly on the double bed, next to several empty boxes of pills. Knight appeared to have been trying to commit suicide. Or was faking it.

The Tuesday before, Price had told his boss that Katherine had gone berserk and grabbed a kitchen knife. He had then woken that night, to see her standing at the end of the bed with the knife. The following day, he took out a court order to keep her away from him and his house.

Then, that evening, Katherine had unusually taken her kids to dinner, telling them: 'I want it to be special.' Sensing something was wrong, her daughter Natasha said: 'I hope you are not going to kill Pricey and yourself.'

BACKGROUND

Born in New South Wales in 1955, Katherine Knight went to work in an abattoir at the age of sixteen. Co-workers remember that she was particularly adept at beheading pigs and had exhibited a perverse fascination with the front end of the production line where the animals' throats were cut. She was so proud of her profession that, wherever she lived, she kept her razor-sharp boning knives hanging above her bed.

In 1973, she met twenty-two-year-old truck-driver David Kellett. They married the following year. On her wedding night, she tried to strangle him because she was not satisfied with his sexual performance. On another occasion, she smashed him in the face with a hot iron when he came home with a six-pack of beer. One morning he awoke to find her sitting on his chest holding a knife to his throat.

'You see how easy it is,' she said. 'Is it true that drivers have different women in every town?'

Fearing for his life, Kellett left. She then left their baby on the railway tracks when a train was due – it was rescued in the nick of time by a local man and she was apprehended swinging an axe at passers-by. She stabbed a policeman, but somehow escaped without charge. When she found out where her husband was, she slashed a woman's face and demanded that she drive her to him. After taking a child hostage, she was admitted to a psychiatric hospital in Morisset.

With Knight under medication, the couple reunited and moved to Queensland together, where she got a job in another meat works. Then in 1984, they split. She moved back to Aberdeen and the abattoir, but soon lost her job because of a back injury. She took up with David Saunders, who complained that she cut up his clothes, smashed up his car, stabbed him with a pair of scissors and cut the throat of his eight-week-old puppy to intimidate him.

Then she dropped Saunders for John Chillingworth. Again the relationship was violent. She smashed his glasses and his false teeth. Along the way she gave birth to a number of children which she lodged with her parents in Aberdeen.

In 1994, she took up with father-of-three John Price.

During questioning, Knight denied having any recollection of what had happened that night, beyond having pleasurable sex, and had no memory of stabbing him. However, the bloodstains showed that he managed to get to the front door before she dragged him back. He died in the hallway. There were thirty-seven stab wounds in his body, puncturing all his major organs.

On assessing the murder scene, a crime scene officer said of John Price:

He's absolutely fighting for his life. The bloke's just had a bonk in the bed when he wakes up, then stab, stab, stab. He's getting up, there is arterial spurting on the robe and the bed, and on the doorway there's a bloodied handprint or swipe on the western side of the door near the dressing table, and blood around the light switch. It looks like he's tried to turn the light switch on. And then all down the hallway they're [bloody handprints] everywhere. And he's almost made it, he's opened the front door, the screen door is shut, there is blood staining, trajectory again, flicking out across the front door, he's almost made it . . . but he wouldn't have survived. He would have been absolutely horrified, terrified – probably terrified more than horrified – trying to get out and all the time being stabbed.

After expertly skinning Price, Katherine had sliced him up and prepared a grisly meal for his children. Next she wrote a series of vindictive and barely literate notes. She had a cup of coffee and a cigarette, then she took a thousand dollars from Price's account at a nearby ATM.

Nevertheless, at trial, she pleaded guilty and was sentenced to life imprisonment without possibility of parole, the first woman in Australia to be given such a sentence.

Crime scene

At 10 a.m. on 1 March 2000, crime scene investigator Detective Senior Constable Peter Muscio visited 84 St Andrews Street. In his report he said:

My attention was drawn to a piece of cooked meat on the rear lawn in front of the white Ford sedan. I made an examination of this piece of meat and collected it for further testing ...
I walked in through the rear door and into the kitchen. Once inside the kitchen I saw a large section of what appeared to be human skin hanging from the top architrave of the doorway leading into the lounge room. This piece of skin extended from the top of the doorway right to the floor and appeared to be an entire human skin. Looking through this doorway into the lounge room I could see a headless and skinless human body. I walked east along the hallway and looked into the entry foyer and saw an extreme amount of blood pooled on the floor. There was also a large amount of blood smearing over the eastern wall of the entry ...

In the kitchen he found:

Just to the right or northern side of the cook top I saw two prepared meals. Each of the meals consisted of two pieces of cooked meat, baked potato, baked pumpkin, zucchini, cabbage, yellow squash and gravy. Underneath each of the meals was a torn section of kitchen paper with a name written on it. The word 'Beaky' was written in blue ink pen on one of the pieces while the word 'Jonathon' was on the other. The pieces of meat appeared on the plates were similar to the piece I collected from the rear lawn ...

STACEY CASTOR

The Black Widow *USA, 2000–05*

Sentencing the 'black widow' to a minimum of 51⅓ years in jail, Judge Joseph Fahey said: 'In my thirty-four years in the criminal justice system as a lawyer and a judge, I have seen serial killers, contract killers, killers of every variety and stripe. But, I have to say, Mrs Castor, you are in a class all by yourself.' Not only had she killed her husbands, she had also tried to kill her daughter so she would take the blame.

S tacey Ruth Daniels was just seventeen when she met the man she would call the love of her life, Michael Wallace. 'I knew five minutes after I met him that I was going to marry him,' she said.

They were soon inseparable. Five years after their first date, they were married. Two years later they had their first child, their daughter, Ashley. Three years later a second daughter named Bree came along. Ashley was hurt that her father made no secret of the fact that he preferred her younger sister, called her 'princess' and 'daddy's little angel'. Stacey tried to compensate by spending more time with Ashley, trying to be her best friend.

Financially, life was hard for a family of four in upstate New York in the 1990s. Stacey worked for an ambulance despatch company, while Michael worked nights as a mechanic. This put a strain on their relationship and there were rumours of affairs.

Towards the end of 1999, Michael began to get ill. His sister-in-law Melanne Keim said he was unsteady on his feet as if he were drunk. The condition dragged on intermittently for six weeks. By

Christmas Eve, he was swollen and puffy, and was coughing a lot. Family members encouraged him to see a doctor.

Ashley, then eleven, remembered the traumatic day in January when her father died.

'He was laying on the couch, making what I thought were funny faces,' she said. 'And all of a sudden, he just sticks his arm up in the air and puts his arm on his side and then his arm just fell down.'

She left him there when she went to pick up Bree from school. When she returned, her father was dead. There was nothing she could have done, but she blamed herself for his death for years afterwards.

The hospital told Stacey that her husband had died of a heart attack. His sister Rosemary Corbett had her doubts.

'The colour of his skin from head to chest was deep, dark purple,' she said. 'It was really weird.'

Nevertheless her request for a post-mortem was blocked by Stacey.

Three years later, Stacey married again. Her second husband was David Castor. She worked as office manager at his business, Liverpool Heating and Air Conditioning. Around two o'clock one afternoon, she called the Onondaga County Sheriff as her husband had not turned up to work. They had had a row the day before and he had locked himself in their bedroom. She had tried calling his cell phone repeatedly, but he had not picked up. She was worried because he was depressed and he kept a gun in the room.

Sergeant Robert Willoughby went to the house. Unable to get any response when he knocked on the bedroom door, he kicked it in. He found David Castor lying naked across the bed, dead. On the nightstand, there was a bottle of apricot brandy and a glass half full of bright green liquid, and lying on the floor next to the bed was a container of antifreeze. Willoughby said he remembered that when he told her, Stacey screamed: 'He's not dead! He's not dead!'

When Detective Dominick Spinelli arrived, Castor said she thought the recent death of his father plus the rising stress of the business may have led her husband to take his own life. While detectives collected the glasses and bottles from the bedroom, Sergeant Willoughby had a look in the kitchen. In the garbage can, he found a turkey baster. It looked brand new, smelled of alcohol and had a few drops of liquid in it.

'I found that very odd,' he said. 'He had no food around. No dirty dishes. No indication that anybody had been cooking or baking. I know he's been drinking. I know alcohol's involved. I know antifreeze was involved.'

This time there was a post-mortem. Antifreeze is difficult to detect, but the medical examiner found telltale calcium oxalate crystals in the kidneys. The sweet-tasting liquid is easy enough to swallow. Even a small amount causes the internal organs to close down. There were also traces of antifreeze on the turkey baster, indicating that it had been fed drip by drip. It is a slow and painful way to die.

During their interview, Castor had told Spinelli that she thought her husband may have chosen that way to die because he had recently watched a documentary on Lynn Turner, who had killed her husband and subsequent partner by poisoning them with antifreeze.

Spinelli, a street-smart cop transplanted from New York, said: 'A sixth sense is something you develop throughout your career. It tells you something ain't right.'

Checking her phone records, he discovered that Castor had made only one phone call to her husband that day. The fingerprints on the glass containing antifreeze turned out to be Stacey Castor's, not David's. And the antifreeze can had no prints on it at all. Nor did the turkey baster – but it did have David Castor's DNA on the tip.

After David Castor was buried next to Michael Wallace, Spinelli persisted with the case. He had Wallace's body disinterred. It too showed signs of the ingestion of ethylene glycol, the toxic ingredient of antifreeze.

Stacey Castor was brought in for questioning. After three hours, she insisted on seeing an attorney. When Ashley discovered that her mother – and 'best friend' – was a murder suspect, she was outraged. Detectives wiretapping her mother's phone heard Ashley telling her mother: 'I wish that I had done this so they would take the focus off you and it would put the focus on me.' These were words that would come back to haunt her.

When Ashley grew hysterical, Stacey came to pick her up from school. Ashley recalled her saying: 'Oh, we've had a hard week, let's just drink.'

She was thrilled.

'What kind of teenager wouldn't think that was awesome,' said Ashley. 'Your parents just gave you permission to drink. Sweet. So I drank with her.'

They drank Watermelon Smirnoff Ice from the bottle. Ashley got sick and her mother gave her a pill and sent her to bed.

The next day when Ashley got home from school, they started drinking again. Her mother gave her a cup of vodka. Though it was mixed with Sprite and orange juice, it tasted strangely bitter.

The next morning when Ashley did not get up to go to school, Bree went to check on her.

'Her mouth was open and her eyes were wide open and they were all glassy,' said Bree Wallace. 'I tried to call her name and she didn't answer me. I screamed for my mom and she came flying.'

Stacey dialled 911, telling the dispatcher: 'I need an ambulance. My daughter, I believe, had taken some pills.' She said that Ashley had downed dozens with a bottle of vodka.

When Bree went back to Ashley's bedroom, she found what appeared to be a suicide note. Typewritten and some 750 words long, it contained a confession to the murder of both Wallace and Castor, giving details only the murderer could know. Ashley's name was at the bottom and it was addressed to her mother, saying: 'Now everyone is going to know what really happened, and they know it wasn't you, it was me.'

Ashley was rushed to hospital in the nick of time and survived. When she came to, she denied taking any pills, or writing a suicide note. Spinelli concluded that her mother was responsible.

'Stacey knew our grip was getting a lot tighter on her,' he said. 'There was really no way out of it besides using her daughter as a scapegoat.'

Castor was arrested at the hospital and charge with the murder of her second husband and the attempted murder of her daughter. Although Stacey's mother continued to believe that Ashley was responsible, there was damning evidence against Stacey. The suicide note had been written on her computer at times when Ashley was at school. The wiretaps recorded the sound of typing when Stacey was on the phone, though she denied using the computer at that time. The note also included the word 'antifree' instead of antifreeze four times. Castor also used the word 'antifree' in an interview, but insisted that she had truncated the word because she had meant to say something else. What's more, the note had Castor's fingerprints on it, not Ashley's.

In court, Castor continued to maintain that Ashley was the murderer, even though she had only been eleven at the time of her father's death. Stacey Castor was found guilty of the second-degree murder of her husband and the attempted second-degree murder of her daughter.

Before passing sentence, John Joseph Fahey said: 'Unlike many defendants who pass through my courtroom, you're not just a danger to the general public you're a danger to the people who love you and are closest to you. I believe that the sentence that I'm about to impose will remove that danger once and for all.'

He sentenced her to the maximum of twenty-five years to life for the murder of David Castor, and another twenty-five years for the attempted murder of Ashley, along with another one year four months to four years for forging David Castor's signature, denying his son by a previous marriage of his inheritance.

Stacey Castor died in Bedford Hills Correctional Facility for Women in Westchester County on 11 June 2016, still protesting her innocence.

The children's testimony

Stacey Castor's eldest daughter Ashley Wallace, with her sister Bree by her side, told the court: 'I never knew what hate was until now. Even though I do hate her, I still love her at the same time. That bothers me, it is so confusing. How can you hate someone and love them at the same time? I just wish that she would say sorry for everything she did, including all the lies. As horrible as it makes me feel, this is goodbye, Mom. As hard as you tried, I survived and I will survive because now I'm surrounded by people that love me. I'm going to do good things in this world despite making me in every sense of the word an orphan.'

David Castor Jr added: 'Your honour, Stacey Castor is a monster and a threat to society. Mr Fitzpatrick said there's a ladder for the level of criminal and she is at the ceiling and this is true, she has created so much pain and death with this family.'

Outside he said it was a struggle to find the right words to describe the woman who had killed his father.

'The amount of pain that Stacey R. Castor put our family through is indescribable and immeasurable,' he said. 'She tortured my dad.'

Ashley told reporters: 'I've cried enough tears about this and I don't want to cry anymore, I just want it all to go away, but I know it will never go away. I have to live with this the rest of my life.'

She had never suspected that her mother could do such evil things. 'Not a day in my life. Never. She was like my best friend, Stacey. Yeah, she really was. And she just ruined that trust.'

Ashley said she had found it difficult to read out her statement condemning her mother in court.

'It was really hard, I was really nervous,' she said. 'I got to speak my mind and I didn't get to do that when I was testifying. But it felt really good at the same time. It did. It was a relief.'

Joining hands with Bree, she said: 'We're just happy that it's over. We really are. Now that I know everybody knows I didn't do it, it's just ten times lighter.'

As for her mother: 'I felt betrayed. Like, she just . . . a bond that you should never break, is a bond between your children and a mother and she completely broke that bond, when she did what she did. I don't want to talk to her ever again. I really don't. I really have nothing to say to her. I'm glad she'll be away for a very long time, and she can't hurt anybody ever again.'

JUANA BARRAZA

The Old Lady Killer *Mexico, 2002–06*

In their search for *El Mataviejitas* – 'The Old Lady Killer' – who was killing women over sixty, the police in Mexico City assumed that the masculine figure dressed in women's clothing witnesses said they had seen leaving the crime scene was a transvestite. It turned out to be a female professional wrestler known as *La Dama del Silencio*.

During the 1980s and 1990s, Barraza toured Mexico in a form of wrestling known as *lucha libre*, or free fighting. The fighters wore masks and had cartoon-character names. They were identified as either *técnicos* – good guys who fought by the rules – or *rudos* – villains who broke them. Interviewed by a TV channel attending a wrestling match a few weeks before her arrest, Barraza described herself as '*rudo* to the core'. She later told the police that she had picked the professional name *La Dama del Silencio* 'because I am quiet and keep myself to myself'.

Fairly low down the rankings, she was getting just 300 to 500 pesos – between $15 and $30 – a fight and began shoplifting and housebreaking to support her children. In 1996, she and a friend began stealing from elderly people. They would dress up as nurses to gain access and steal when they got inside. However, her friend's lover was a corrupt cop who charged Barraza 12,000 pesos not to arrest her for a job she had done alone.

When Barraza retired from the ring in the year 2000, her financial situation grew worse. A spate of brutal murders of elderly people began in Mexico City. The press dubbed the killer *El Mataviejitas*, assuming it was a male. However, the police denied that there was a serial killer on the loose.

The first murder associated with Barraza was that of María de la Luz González Anaya on 25 November 2002. Once Barraza entered her apartment, González made comments that Barraza considered derogatory. Infuriated, she beat González before strangling her to death with her bare hands. After three months, she killed again.

A year later, the police had enough evidence and witness statements to conclude that a serial killer was at work. The killer was a tall person with rough features who was posing as a city council nurse or social worker to gain the victims' trust, they said. In December 2003, the police released a wanted poster with two eyewitness sketches of the *Mataviejitas* – one slightly feminine and another more masculine.

Mexico City police had an eyewitness account that described the killer as 'a man, dressed as a woman, or a robust woman, dressed in white, height between 1.70 and 1.75 metres [5ft 2in–5ft 7in], robust complexion, light brown, oval face, wide cheeks, blonde hair, delineated eyebrows, [and] approximately forty-five years old'. The Mexican Department of Justice also developed a psychological profile after examining cases of serial killers that targeted elderly women in France and Spain, which specified that the killer was 'a man with homosexual preferences, victim of childhood physical abuse, [who] lived surrounded by women, he could have had a grandmother or lived with an elderly person, has resentment to that feminine figure, and possesses great intelligence'. Consequently, the police announced that they were looking for a homosexual man, who was 'transvestite or transgendered'. They then arrested forty-nine transvestite prostitutes who were all then released when their fingerprints didn't match those at the crime scenes.

Meanwhile Barraza continued approaching her victims on the

street or knocking on their door, pretending to be a city council nurse or social worker. At first, she had simply worn white clothes, but later acquired a nurse's uniform. She would gain their trust by offering them a massage or help in obtaining medicines and benefits. If her victims were distracted, she strangled them directly. If not, she would beat them, using moves she had learned in her wrestling career. Though she carried a bag with medical equipment, she usually strangled her victims manually or with a ligature taken from the victim's own home, which she would leave at the crime scene. Then she would rob them.

The killing of eighty-two-year-old Carmen Camila González Miguel on 28 September 2005 – mother of prominent Mexican criminologist Luis Rafael Moreno González – spurred the police into launching a special operation under the name of *Operación Parques y Jardines* – 'Operation Parks and Gardens'. Patrols in the areas where the killer was active increased and pamphlets were distributed advising old ladies to be wary of strangers. The police even paid elderly women to act as bait in park areas.

On 25 January 2006, Barraza was seen by a tenant as she left the apartment of landlady Ana María de los Reyes Alfaro, whom she had just murdered, and was arrested by a passing police patrol. A search of her home revealed a trophy room complete with newspaper clippings of the murders and mementoes taken from the victims, along with an altar to Jesús Malverde and Santa Muerte, two folk saints often honoured by Mexican criminals.

Barraza was charged with thirty murders – though it was thought that she had committed many more. She was found guilty of sixteen, plus twelve robberies, where she could be tied to the crime scene by fingerprint evidence. She was sentenced to 759 years in prison and is due to be paroled in 2058, at the age of one hundred.

BACKGROUND

Juana Dayanara Barraza Samperio was born in rural Hidalgo, Mexico, in 1957. Her mother was an alcoholic prostitute who left her father, a policeman, soon after she was born. Suffering a troubled relationship with her mother, Juana barely spoke as an infant and never learnt to read or write.

When she was eleven, her mother gave her to a man in exchange for three beers. He sexually abused her and she suffered miscarriages at the age of thirteen and sixteen. After her mother died of cirrhosis of the liver, Juana left for Mexico City. There she had four children from a series of failed marriages. Her eldest son died in a gang shooting at the age of twenty-four.

Juana Barraza seems to have blamed her many misfortunes on her mother and this is assumed to be the motivation for her murder spree.

IRINA GAIDAMACHUK

Satan in a Skirt *Russia, 2002–10*

To friends, family and neighbours, Irina Gaidamachuk appeared to be a perfectly normal wife and mother. She drank heavily and lived on the breadline – not uncommon in Russia – but she was kind, charming and seemingly harmless. Then it was discovered that, over eight years, she had killed at least seventeen victims, smashing their heads in with an axe, a hammer, an iron and even a bronze bust of Lenin.

Her victims were between sixty-one and eighty-nine years of age. They were bludgeoned to death with repeated blows for the small amounts of cash they had in their purses. Sometimes she would glean as little as £20 and only gathered a total of some £1,000 from her victims.

The police fingerprinted 15,000 women, questioned 3,000 witnesses, conducted more than 2,000 forensic examinations and travelled as far as the Central Asian republic of Turkmenistan, 1,300 miles away, in pursuit of leads. In 2008 they arrested another woman named Marina Valeeva. Under pressure from the authorities, she confessed to the murders of several of Gaidamachuk's elderly victims. She turned out to be innocent, but she was held for several months.

Police finally got their break when one of the victims survived an attack and was able to help police draw an artist's impression. Neighbours recognized the drawing as the woman who had painted the victims' flats shortly before they were killed. The net closed in on Irina Gaidamachuk. When she was finally caught it was found that fingerprints at three murder scenes in 2010 matched those at an earlier crime scene.

BACKGROUND

Born in 1972 in the town of Nyagan in Western Siberia, Irina became addicted to alcohol at an early age. At twenty-one she had a baby daughter named Alina, which she handed over to a state-run orphanage. Escaping her parents, she moved five hundred miles away to Krasnoufimsk in the Urals, 760 miles from Moscow. With her husband Yuri, Irina had two children. Her murder spree began in the towns surrounding Krasnoufimsk in 2002, when Gaidamachuk was thirty.

Yuri's mother, Valentina Kuznetsova, said that she knew all along that her daughter-in-law had a drink problem. She would also behave strangely sometimes – pretending to take a call and speaking to herself on the phone – but said she had never thought her capable of murder. Indeed, even when Irina was arrested she did not believe it. 'We're all in a state of shock,' she said, 'still hoping the police have made a mistake.'

Yuri, who had moved in with a new partner, said: 'I lived with her for fourteen years but never suspected anything.'

Their twelve-year-old daughter Anastasia, who lived with her mother, was equally disbelieving: 'She was always good to me and helped me do my homework and even write poetry. I don't believe what people are saying about her can be true,' she said.

One friend said: 'I simply cannot believe Irina is a mass murderer. She was a kind and gentle mother, always eager to help.'

Confessing to the police, Irina said: 'I did it for money. I just wanted to be a normal mum, but I had a craving for drink. My husband Yuri wouldn't give me money for vodka.'

However, she also told the police that her main motive was to send money to Alina, the child she had sent to the orphanage. Detectives believed she felt guilty at having abandoned her daughter.

Shortly before she was captured, in a single week, she killed three women living in the same street in Krasnoufimsk. She picked on elderly women who lived alone. The police said she had got hold of a regional list of pensioners and set out to befriend them by offering to redecorate their flats or carry out household chores. For several days, she would watch her potential victims to find out when they left home, where they went, and whether they were visited by any relatives. On another occasion, after she had smashed an eighty-two-year-old woman's skull, she set her apartment on fire in an attempt to destroy the evidence.

Gaidamachuk was found to be mentally competent and was convicted of seventeen counts of murder and one of attempted murder. She was sentenced to twenty years in prison – meaning that she would only be the age of her youngest victim when she was released. The judge said he had deducted five years from the maximum sentence of twenty-five years because she was a mother.

While her lawyer demanded greater leniency, saying he would appeal the sentence, the families of the victim were outraged. One family member said: 'It's little more than one year for each murder. She never deserves to be freed.'

The investigation

The police came under criticism over the length of time it took to apprehend Irina Gaidamachuk.

'It's scandalous that it took eight years to catch the killer,' said Elena Golovenkina, whose sixty-six-year-old mother was murdered in 2002 in a rain of blows from the statue of Lenin.

The investigation took eight years because the police thought they were looking for a man.

'She's an exceptionally brutal woman,' said one of the detectives on the case. 'I was convinced we were dealing with a man. After all, how could a woman smash a head with twenty-four blows? For a while, when witnesses began talking about a woman, we even suspected a man dressed up as a woman.

'She said she'd lost count of how many people she'd killed after the tenth murder. She's very cold-blooded but also charming and even attractive. She even tried flirting during our questioning.'

After getting away with her murder spree for so long, she had eventually grown careless.

'At some point, Gaidamachuk decided she would never be caught, and started searching for victims among the people she knew,' investigator Kirill Melenkov told *Komsomolskaya Pravda*. 'Her last victim hired her to make repairs. That's how we managed to find the killer. She also started leaving notes, "Be home at 11.00, a social worker will visit." A simple handwriting test helped identify the murderer.'

JOANNA DENNEHY

Peterborough Ditch Murders *England, 2013*

The first time wild-child Joanna Dennehy killed – her flatmate – she immediately got a taste for murder. That same year, in 2013, she went on to kill two more men she knew, dumping their bodies in the countryside near Peterborough, and began to hunt strangers. With her boyfriend, she wanted to be a modern-day version of Bonnie and Clyde – though she did not kill in the course of robberies, but did it just for fun.

In 2013, Joanna Dennehy was looking for a room to rent, when she came across a prospective landlord, forty-nine-year-old Kevin Lee. His business partner Paul Creed recalled: 'She told us a story that she had killed her father due to her father raping her and having his child and losing the child ... She also showed us multiple scars on her arms and stomach.' But despite hearing this, and Creed's reticence, Lee decided to give her a chance. She lived rent free in return for looking after his properties.

She first made threats about her landlord Lee when her boyfriend, seven-foot-two Gary Richards, aka Stretch, did some work for Lee, but had not been paid. Complaining of harassment, she said she would 'f***ing kill him'.

Then, the murders of the residents began. Thirty-one-year-old housemate Lukasz Slaboszewski believed he was going to have sex with Dennehy when he received texts luring him to a flat she had access to. Instead, he was stabbed in the heart, his body dumped in a wheelie bin.

Fifty-six-year-old Falklands veteran John Chapman was high on drink and drugs when Dennehy came on to him. He too was stabbed to death and his body dumped. Lee had been trying to evict these two men, both unemployed, at the time, but had not envisaged the methods Dennehy would use.

Lee seemingly became Joanna's lover. But not for long. She sent him a text asking him to meet her, saying that she wanted to dress him up and rape him. She stabbed him in the heart, then dressed him in a black sequined dress before dumping his body in a ditch near Newborough, Cambridgeshire. He was found face down with the buttocks exposed in what the prosecution described as a 'deliberately engineered . . . act of post-death humiliation', adding: 'The way in which his body was dumped was part of the playing out of [Dennehy's] sexual and sadistic motivation.'

After Lee's murder, she sang down the phone the Britney Spears track 'Oops I Did It Again' to a friend. Dennehy and Stretch then posed for photographs celebrating the killings. They also torched Lee's Ford Mondeo.

Lee's wife was already suspicious of the affair. She noticed that a number appeared frequently on her husband's telephone bills and rang it. The number was Dennehy's. The police used it later to show that she was in the vicinity of the car when it was set on fire.

EVIL, PURE AND SIMPLE

In an interview for the Crime and Investigation Channel, Dennehy's mother Kathleen said her daughter was a sensitive child when growing up. But Dennehy started to change in her mid-teens, skipping school, drinking, taking drugs and dating a man named John Treanor who was five years her senior. She had two daughters with him.

Seeing video of her daughter after she was arrested, Kathleen added: 'When I saw this footage of Jo it was like somebody I didn't know. She's standing there being charged, smiling and laughing, that's not the kind, loving Jo that was our baby.'

Treanor said: 'I really believe Jo is evil, pure and simple, that is why I took the girls as far away from her as possible.'

He moved to the north of England after suffering abuse and violence at her hand.

'Jo was a nightmare,' said a neighbour. 'She was trouble from the start. She hit him all the time. He would have black eyes and marks on his face.'

Like so much of what Dennehy said, the allegation of her father raping her was not true. She told another acquaintance that she had served thirteen years in prison for killing her father because he had been sexually abusing her since the age of six. Dennehey had indeed served time, but it was for theft and drugs offences. She was also on probation for assault and owning a dangerous dog.

Only three weeks before the murders, she had attacked Carla White, who shared a flat with Stretch. After shaking hands, Joanna Dennehy told Carla to 'f*** off'. When Carla took offence, Dennehy put her hands around her throat. Only when White grabbed a hammer did Dennehy let go of her throat. The encounter seems to have in part piqued Lee's interest in Dennehy. He compared her to Uma Thurman in *Kill Bill*.

A few days after the murders, Dennehy told Stretch: 'I want my fun. I need you to get my fun.' He drove her to Hereford where she stabbed two dog-walkers, Robin Bereza and John Rogers. An acquaintance, Mark Lloyd, was unwittingly brought along with them for the ride. He was terrified of Joanna Dennehy: 'If she had told me to put my head through the windscreen, I would have done,' he said.

When Lloyd discovered that the couple were wanted by the police, he said: 'I thought it was Gary who done the murders because he's 7ft 2in and looks like Herman off *The Munsters*. She looks like butter wouldn't melt until she opens her bloody mouth.'

When they spotted dog-walker Bereza, Lloyd said: 'I thought she was going to mug him but then it twigged on me. I thought: "You just want blood."'

He added: 'She wanted to be like Bonnie and Clyde. She wanted nine victims.'

Surviving the attack, Bereza later said: 'I felt a blow to my right shoulder. I turned around and saw this lady, she just stared straight through me. I kicked her and made contact. It had no impact on her. She just came straight towards me. I ran into the road. I put my hand to my jacket and saw all this blood. She tried to come for me again, I kicked her again; she still didn't react.'

The attack on Rogers was even more horrific. First, he felt a punch in the back, like a neighbour or a friend was messing about and suddenly she started stabbing him in the chest.

Rogers recalled: 'I said: "Just leave me alone please, please can you leave me alone", but she didn't. She didn't seem to be showing any emotion. She didn't seem to be enjoying herself. She just seemed like she was going about business.'

Rogers said he fell to the ground but Dennehy continued unrelenting: 'I was just waiting for it to stop. There was loads and loads of blood on the floor on the ground. As I lay there I thought, This is where I'm going to die.'

He had been stabbed forty times in his arms, chest, stomach and back when Dennehy left him for dead.

After two days on the run, Dennehy and Stretch were captured by two armed officers when their green Vauxhall Astra was spotted parked in The Oval area of Hereford. Surrendering to the police, Stretch told the officers: 'I suppose I'm Britain's "most wanted".' In fact, that dubious accolade belonged to Dennehy.

In custody, she told a psychiatrist: 'I killed to see if I was as cold as I thought I was. Then it got moreish and I got a taste for it.'

In the Old Bailey, Dennehy unexpectedly pleaded guilty to the three murders – though she had bragged that she had killed eight – along with two counts of attempted murder and preventing the lawful and decent burial of her murder victims. She was sentenced to life with a whole-life tariff after writing to the judge saying she felt no remorse for the killings. Dennehy was only the third woman to receive that sentence. The other two were Myra Hindley and Rosemary West.

Gary Stretch (formerly Richards) was found guilty of two counts of attempted murder, while Leslie Layton, another house-mate of Dennehy's, was convicted of perverting the course of justice and preventing lawful burials. Stretch was sentenced to life, with a minimum term of nineteen years, and Layton got fourteen years.

Dennehy and Stretch exchanged letters from jail, confirming their love for each other.

Dennehy sued the authorities over being kept in solitary con-finement in jail, but the case was dismissed after it was revealed that she had been plotting to escape by cutting off a guard's finger to open the biometric locks in the prison.

TAMARA SAMSONOVA

Granny Ripper *Russia, 1995–2015*

Sixty-eight-year-old Tamara Samsonova was arrested after local dogs found the limbs of her friend, seventy-nine-year-old Valentina Ulanova, in the undergrowth near her block of flats in St Petersburg. When CCTV footage was checked, Samsonova was seen going in and out of her friend's flat seven times carrying body parts in bags and a saucepan containing her head. Her diaries revealed that she had killed up to eleven people over twenty years.

Tamara Samsonova was Valentina Ulanov's carer and killed her after a quarrel over an unwashed cup; Samsonova put drugs in a salad and once Ulanov was unconscious, Samsonova cut her up with a hacksaw while she was still alive.

When dogs sniffed out human remains, the police began a major manhunt. A social worker reported Mrs Ulanova missing after Samsonova refused her entry to the apartment.

'I came home and put the whole pack of phenazepam – fifty pills – into her Olivier salad,' Samsonova later confessed to the police. 'She liked it very much. I woke up after 2 a.m. and she was lying on the floor. So I started cutting her to pieces. It was hard for me to carry her to the bathroom, she was fat and heavy. I did everything at the kitchen where she was lying.'

She wrapped body parts in curtains and put them in plastic bags before dumping them near a pond in Dimitrova Street. Her hips and legs only made it as far as the back yard. The head and hands were boiled in a large saucepan. These have not been found by the police. Nor have the internal organs. It is thought that they were thrown in the garbage skip, which was collected the following Saturday, though Samsonova may have eaten them.

She made a total of seven trips outside carrying body parts. CCTV showed a figure in a blue raincoat dragging bags that left a trail of blood.

The dismembered torso of a man – minus his arms, legs and head – was found in the same street twelve years earlier. The victim's business card and other evidence linking Samsonova to the murder were found in her flat.

Among her collection of books on black magic and astrology, detectives found diaries whose entries were in Russian, French and English. They included an account of the murder of two of her former lodgers.

'I killed my tenant Volodya, cut him to pieces in the bathroom with a knife, put the pieces of his body in plastic bags and threw them away in the different parts of Frunzensky district,' she wrote.

A forty-four-year-old native of Norilsk, Sergei Potynavin was killed after an argument on 6 September 2003. She then dismembered his body and dumped the body parts in plastic bags.

Such chilling confessions were found among more mundane entries saying that she had slept badly, skipped eating or taken her medicine. One read: 'I woke at 5 a.m. I am drinking coffee. Then I do work around the house.' It went on to say that she went out to buy marshmallow. Another entry makes clear she liked living with Mrs Ulanova, whom she called Valya, even saying: 'I love Valya.'

The diaries also include poems, songs, reflections on life and descriptions of her victim's tattoos. Other entries told of how she ate some of her victims.

The police also found a knife and a saw, and there were spots of blood in the bathroom. The former hotel worker admitted eleven murders without giving details. It was thought that she had indeed eaten some body parts from her victims, showing a particular penchant for gouging out their lungs and eating them.

It was feared that she had also disposed of her husband, whom she reported missing in 2005. She told the police that he had met another woman. At the time he disappeared, neighbour Marina Krivenko recalled: 'We had some coffee in her kitchen, and we chatted. She already looked strange then. She told me about her husband, that he left home and did not come back. And at that moment I noticed some kind of pleasure in Tamara's eyes.'

Samsonova's mother-in-law also disappeared and she admitted to an old school friend, sixty-seven-year-old Anna Batalina, that she was suspected of killing her. Mrs Batalina was also thought to have been in danger after Samsonova flew into a rage with her, screaming: 'I'll kill you. I'll cut you to pieces. I will throw the pieces out for the dogs. Don't make me angry.'

Mrs Krivenko had known Samsonova for fifteen years and said that she was very interested in the bloodthirsty killer Andrei Chikatilo.

'She gathered information about him and how he committed his murders,' the neighbour said.

For years she had boasted to friends that, one day 'I will be popular and famous.' She told them she would one day cause a 'sensation' without explaining how or why.

Mrs Krivenko reported other eccentric behaviour.

'I came to live here with my husband,' she said. 'I used to go to Tamara's flat and call from her phone. She looked a lot better fifteen years ago, and her flat too was a lot more attractive than now. She looked after her appearance, and had this weird habit of sitting topless with her back to the window, making sure that her silhouette was seen by the neighbours.'

Apparently, Mr Krivenko found this rather appealing. Mrs Krivenko also admitted lending Samsonova a hacksaw some years earlier, which she never returned.

Despite facing the death penalty, Samsonova was more concerned about the publicity her arrest had attracted. She told reporters: 'I knew you would come. It's such a disgrace for me, all the city will know.'

However, she bore no hostility towards newsmen, blowing a kiss to them. She refused to take the charges seriously. When the judge Roman Chebotaryov asked her to address the court, she said: 'It's stuffy in here, can I go out?'

She seemed to be relieved to have been caught, telling the judge: 'I was getting ready for this court action for dozens of years. It was all done deliberately ... There is no way to live. With this last murder I closed the chapter.'

The judge said: 'I am asked to detain you. What do you think?'

'You decide, your honour,' she replied. 'After all, I am guilty and I deserve punishment.'

When she was told that she would remain in custody, she beamed and clapped her hands.

While admitting to murdering Mrs Ulanova and others, Samsonova refused to co-operate with police over other suspected killings. Although the police did not rule out further charges, without finding the body parts, prosecution would be problematic.

'We may never know the extent of this granny's killings,' one source close to the investigation said.

After the hearing, Samsonova was taken under guard on a high-security train nearly a thousand miles to a psychiatric prison hospital in Kazan, capital of Tatarstan, for assessment. This was where Josef Stalin's secret police used to lock up political prisoners. It is now called the Kazan Psychiatric Hospital of Special Purpose with Intensive Guarding.

Andrei Chikatilo

Between 1978 and 1990, Chikatilo, aka 'The Rostov Ripper', killed between fifty-two and fifty-six children, getting sexual satisfaction from their brutal murders and eating their sexual organs. He also chopped out their tongues, burst their eardrums and gouged out their eyes which he feared had logged his image. After his arrest, he confessed fifty-six murders to a psychiatrist.

Judged to be sane and fit to stand trial, he was kept in an iron cage in the courtroom. Found guilty of fifty-two of the fifty-three murders he was charged with, he was executed with a single bullet behind the right ear.

Samsonova was not the only killer who modelled themselves on Chikatilo. The 'Chessboard Maniac' Alexander Pichushkin set out to beat Chikatilo and kill one person for every square on the chess board. He was jailed for life in 2007 for killing sixty-two people, mainly in Bitza Park in Moscow.

The following year sixty-two-year-old ex-detective Serhiy Tkach was convicted by a Ukrainian court in 2008 of twenty-nine murders and eleven attempted murders. The Russian-born monster claimed to have killed up to two hundred people over a quarter of a century. His motive, he said, was revenge on women and simple sexual pleasure. He also boasted: 'I'm not a man, I'm a beast. Same as Chikatilo.'

Penza cannibal Alexander Bychkov manically stabbed his victims in the same way as Chikatilo, whom he named as one of his idols along with Hitler. Arrested at the age of twenty-three in 2012, he had already killed eleven elderly men and eaten them. His mother said she saw him cutting out stories about Chikatilo from the newspapers and pasting them in his scrapbook.

Siberian slaughterer Mikhail Popkov, a former cop, proudly compared himself to Chikatilo, according to the local prosecutor. In 2015, he was convicted of killing twenty-two but was under investigation for another thirty-plus murders.